The Prosperity
EQUATION

The Prosperity EQUATION

The Entrepreneur's Road Map to Wealth

James A. Ziegler

PEACH STATE PRESS
NORCROSS, GEORGIA

Although the author and publisher have made every effort to ensure the accuracy and completeness of information contained in this book, we assume no responsibility for errors, inaccuracies, omissions, or any inconsistency herein. Any slights of people, places, or organizations are unintentional.

First printing 2001

ISBN 0-9705454-3-6

LCCN 00-136408

ATTENTION CORPORATIONS, UNIVERSITIES, COLLEGES, AND PROFESSIONAL ORGANIZATIONS: Quantity discounts are available on bulk purchases of this book for educational, gift purposes, or as premiums for increasing magazine subscriptions or renewals. Special books or book excerpts can also be created to fit specific needs. For information, please contact Peach State Press, 1244 Beaver Ruin Road, #300, Norcross, GA 30093; ph 770-921-4440.

Dedicated to my loving family,
Debbie and Zach,
who stuck it out through the hard times and
lived every moment of the adventure with me.
Everything I've done, I did it for us.

Contents

Part One of
The Prosperity
EQUATION

Get Your Mind Right!

Why did I write this book?

I have always wanted to write a book that was easy to read
and filled with information that would immediately change the
quality of the readers' lives forever. As thoughts and ideas poured
out of my mind, I have made an honest effort to capture them
on these pages before they evaporated and were lost.

The Land of Opportunity. We live in a country where virtually everyone has the constitutional right to become wealthy and
to pursue happiness, that is, if they really want it badly enough
to go for it.

With so much abundance all around us, why are so many
people living in poverty? Why do so many people feel they are
helpless and there is no way to escape their situation?

For years I have meditated and considered those questions.
There was a time in my life when I was searching for answers,
which then became obvious. It wasn't a gradual awakening; it
was more like being knocked down by a bolt of lightning. Suddenly, everything became crystal clear. I realized why so many
people were missing pieces of the puzzle, why so many never

seem to put it all together. I called this revelation the Prosperity Equation.

The Prosperity Equation is a sincere effort to reveal to you the step-by-step journey that has taken me from desolation to success. In these pages I've attempted to quantify thought processes as well as those events I experienced as my life progressed from despair to affluence. Every page has been carefully designed to show you ways to duplicate my successes.

Most of the people I have known throughout my life are not living their dreams. No matter where they are in their lives, things haven't turned out the way they thought they would. And now for many of them, time is running out. So many people seem to wake up from a coma somewhere around middle age and suddenly realize they are facing a crisis. If they are ever going to make it happen at all, then it had better happen quickly. Most Baby Boomers are going into their senior years facing a severe shortage of funds. Looking at the next ten years, we will be dealing with more than ninety million seniors reaching retirement age. That compares to approximately thirty million retirees today. Many of the people I have cared about all of my life are destined to die broke.

No matter who you are—regardless of your background—there are no limits and no boundaries. Virtually anyone can enjoy success, wealth, and prosperity. You must be willing to open your mind and accept change. If you can embrace the elements of the Equation and incorporate its principles into your life's patterns, your life will change dramatically.

The Prosperity Equation is not the inane babbling of some get-rich wannabe ranting about some kind of get-rich-quick scheme. I am a successful, working executive who started with nothing and built my companies and wealth with the very principles I will outline here. There are no hidden agendas. All you must do is use these principles.

When I first made the conscious decision to become wealthy, it was necessary to take a realistic look at myself and eliminate any of the excuses I might have been hanging onto that might be used to justify failure. I wasn't born to wealthy parents and I didn't have an advanced education. My education came from the streets. Like so many people in today's society, for the first thirty-five years of my life I was just sort of flopping around without direction like a fish out of water. Like many successful people I have known, it took an explosive, catastrophic event in my life to shake me up enough to get my life moving in a positive direction. Like so many others, I needed a catalyst to light the fire, to become focused and motivated.

I will readily concede there are many people who are wealthier and smarter and a whole lot better looking than I am; and I suppose too there are many rich people who are uglier, stupider, and less charming. Whoever said any of this was supposed to be fair? It's not so much about who you are as it is about what you've done. It's not about where you started as much as it's about where you're going.

I admit, there are thousands—perhaps millions—of people who are wealthier than I will ever hope to be. (Take Bill Gates, for instance. In ten minutes he makes more money than my lifetime net worth!) But everyone has to be positioned somewhere in the food chain of prosperity. By this measurement, I am doing much better than most. You'd have to place me very close to the very top, within a fraction of one percent, if the net worth of every human being on the planet were listed in ascending order. The reason I feel compelled to point this out is because I have read hundreds of books on how to get rich that were written by people who obviously weren't, never have been, and probably never will be. The Prosperity Equation is written from personal experience, and it's about how to reach higher levels of living extremely well.

This book is really not about me at all. Although there are many parts of the book when I will be talking about some of the events that happened to my family and me as I developed my business and solidified my philosophies, these are only intended to be parables. Rod Stewart had a hit back in the seventies titled *Every Picture Tells a Story*. Well, in this case, every story tells a picture. Each of the examples relating to the events and struggles we endured, back when my wife and I were building the businesses, is designed to illustrate a picture in your mind. I will only relate to you those stories with a purpose to serve as an example of a point I am trying to hammer home. Like you, I am also still on the journey.

There are many ways to become wealthy. I certainly don't claim to know all of them. Let's start with the fact that very few of the world's wealthiest people became wealthy through their investments. My observation is that the stock market is something that generally makes a lot of money for some people after they already became wealthy doing something else. In other words, I believe the stock market is a vehicle where the rich get richer by leveraging their existing wealth.

One of the cornerstone pillars of the Prosperity Equation is to reinvest your money back into the business. Although investments rarely create a person's initial fortune, you have to develop discipline and control when handling money. I have a saying that is often repeated in my Prosperity seminars: "Success leads to excess!" One of the most dynamic concepts in wealth building is the power of compound interest.

Some of the wealthiest people throughout history were great inventors like Henry Ford and Thomas Edison. If you've just patented a revolutionary scientific breakthrough, then you are already destined to be wealthy and famous. Maybe you own the rights to a drug that will reverse the aging process and restore lost youth. If that's the case, then you're already going to be rich. It's automatic. Put the book down. Relax! The game is over. You won! Forget about it! Go play!

Or maybe you're an incredible athlete or talented actor who is destined to be discovered and signed up for some unbelievable amount of money. Once again, congratulations, you don't need this book.

Unfortunately, most of us are not great actors, singers, or athletes. When it comes to Tom Cruise, Britney Spears, Tiger Woods, and Michael Jordan, there are only so many out there. It seems like there's only one Muhammad Ali for each generation and the Beatles phenomenon only happens occasionally.

For me, the only answer, the only avenue for escaping my circumstances, was to start my own business. As a result, I am now the president of three extremely profitable corporations with seven-digit revenues and an incredibly lavish lifestyle.

Let me make an attempt to paint the whole picture for you. Make no mistake, the Prosperity Equation is about how to become wealthy by starting and growing your own business. It is a formula that will allow you to achieve freedom and personal choices, to take control of your destiny. The Prosperity Equation starts out examining the philosophies and mind-sets of success and then transitions into the specifics of how to start and grow an entrepreneurial business. In the pages to follow, I will take you on a journey from the initial mind-set, through the skills and disciplines, to the nuts-and-bolts processes of starting or growing your business.

This is not intended to be light reading. The purpose of the Prosperity Equation is to create emotions within you. I want to help focus your vision and cause you to develop a new desire and intensity. Reread and study every chapter before you move on, and don't move on until you are absolutely certain you have mastered the concepts.

Important aspects of the Equation are advertising, marketing, and sales. Through the years I've studied thousands of hopefuls who started new businesses and ultimately failed. Even though they had the desire to succeed, they just didn't get the rest of the Equation. Success is a thought process! If you can just get your mind right, then you will have mastered three-quarters of the entire equation. It has been my experience that most people who fail and never try again have weaknesses of character, attitude, or determination.

I would like to share with you the strategies and techniques that have made me successful. Am I saying this is the one and the only way to become successful or wealthy? Absolutely not! The Prosperity Equation is meant to be a road map to guide you along the route to financial success, a blueprint for building wealth. Along the way, I hope you will discover personal freedom and a great quality of life. Just as there are many different roads leading to any destination on a physical map of your state or your hometown, there are also many different routes leading to personal prosperity. I am writing this book outlining the one route to success I know best. It is the only route I know.

The Prosperity Equation is not only an outline of what has worked for me, but it has also worked for many of my friends and seminar students. It is, however, only one of the ways to get there. It is certainly not the only way and, even once you know the way, there are no guarantees or assurances you'll make it. Only you know whether or not you've got what it takes to stick it out and make it all of the way to the end of the journey.

The Prosperity Equation is not just a formula for achieving the quantifiable goals of wealth and success; it is also about the freedom wealth affords to achieve a great lifestyle and peace of mind.

Since the core focus of the Prosperity Equation is directed toward owning your own business and being your own boss, we will spend a lot of time discussing the nuts-and-bolts business processes of wealth building. If you were a soldier fighting in a war, you wouldn't go into battle if you were untrained and out-of-shape. You'd be killed. Well, guess what? This isn't any different. It's a war out there and if you decide this is what you really want to do, you must be prepared. It requires study and planning as well as psychological preparation to start and grow a successful business. You've got to be emotionally prepared for what is about to happen.

As you read deeper into these pages, you'll discover this theme will be repeated many times, in many forms, until it sinks deep into the permanent recesses of your subconscious mind. The Prosperity Equation is all about focus and mind-set. It's all about developing an attitude and a philosophy that will lead to your personal growth and development.

I hope, as you read on, you'll start to think of me as your personal trainer who is pushing you hard, stretching your personal limits as you move toward your destination. Maybe I am a drill instructor and this is boot camp. Regardless, my goal is to lead you to achieving your personal goals of wealth and prosperity. I intend to be tough on you.

As I begin to break down the fundamentals of the Prosperity Equation, you'll quickly realize they are interwoven; each principle is dependent upon the other. In other words, you can't pick and choose which ideas and philosophies you want to embrace and which you wish to ignore. The Prosperity Equation is a total package, an-all-or-nothing proposition. It's like one of those magnificent old Greek temples, if you start tearing out the pillars, the whole building will collapse. Well, some things simply can't be modified or changed if you expect them to remain effective. If you are going to have the incredible quality of life you've been dreaming about, you must realize it doesn't come without a personal commitment. If becoming wealthy was easy, everyone would already be there.

It is not necessarily all about becoming filthy rich either. There are many levels of personal prosperity, wealth, and success. This is the Prosperity Equation.

Quantifying the Equation

Have you ever noticed there are some people who seem to have a charisma that attracts others to them? Couldn't exactly put your finger on it but there was just "something" about them. In school, they were the ones who were always popular. You just liked being around them. Did you ever meet a salesperson you really liked doing business with? Of course you have.

What are the traits and habits that make people successful in their lives and businesses? Why are some people destined to become millionaires when others can barely make it until the end of each month? Well, I am about to share with you an incredible formula for realizing wealth and success. But don't expect to immediately appreciate the awesome power of the Prosperity Equation. It won't all come together for you until you have read all of it. The message will only become clear when you arrive at the last words of the last page. This is one of those books you will reread many times, and every time something new will come out of it.

Life is a puzzle and it takes many pieces to complete the picture. That's the Prosperity Equation. I have dedicated my entire life (up until now anyway) studying the traits and habits of successful and wealthy business people. After reading the book *Think and Grow Rich,* written by Napoleon Hill, I learned the dynamic concept of studying the characteristics of winners and then modeling myself after them. It occurred to me that all of the successful people I knew had four common characteristics:

1. Attitude   3. Work ethic
2. Desire   4. Competency

The four basic dynamic concepts, the four cornerstone pillars of the Prosperity Equation are:

1. Attitude   3. Work ethic
2. Desire   4. Competency

That's all there is to it. It's so simplistic. There isn't anything else. Those words standing alone have very little impact until you realize, if you truly possessed all of those qualities, you would already be a millionaire. If you are not a millionaire, I suggest that, perhaps, at least one of those pieces is missing from your personal puzzle.

Now relax. I've only given you part of the equation. There's more.

I know, I just said that's all there is and now I am saying there's more. Well, sort of. To become successful and, ultimately, to become wealthy, there are some other peripheral philosophies and habits you must also master to complete the Equation. These are like the moons revolving around the planets. They tug and pull and have an effect on the gravity of the Equation. These peripherals will determine the degree of success you will achieve.

These peripheral concepts can all be subcategorized as subheadings of one or more of the four basic cornerstone elements of the Equation.

I do not expect you to fully grasp the significance of these concepts right now, in this early stage of the experience. I just wanted to lay them out early on so you can recognize them as they appear, over and over again, in the text and the stories.

Study the rest of the Equation, listed below, and spend a few moments thinking about what these things might mean before you continue.

- Gather people
- Define your vision
- Leverage other people's experience
- See change as a challenge
- Make quick and accurate decisions
- Have a lasting and meaningful relationship
- Saturate your mind with success
- Know God
- Have honor
- Invest your money back into the business
- See each person as an individual
- Embrace technology
- Manage multiple projects

All of the core cornerstone principles of the Equation, as well as the fine-tuned peripherals, will be continually interwoven throughout the text and stories that lie ahead. As you read on, from time to time, put the book down and reflect on how these principles apply to you and your life. Examine your dreams, schemes, and desires and compare them to reality. Most importantly, consider what adjustments and changes you will need to incorporate into your life if you intend to pursue the Prosperity Equation.

Why I've chosen to write this book in several parts

As you read the first chapters of the Prosperity Equation, the message revolves around getting your mind right. Before we dive into the specifics of starting a new business or growing an existing business, I ask that you tear down all of the facades and excuses you might be hiding behind. Take a realistic look at yourself. In these initial chapters, we are going to examine your attitude, desire, philosophies, and work ethic. This is the same material I teach in my prosperity seminars, and I can tell you from experience, most people do not look forward to having to face themselves with their defenses down. If you're up to it, read on. Bear in mind, I never promised that everything you are going to discover about yourself is necessarily going to be exactly the way you would like it to be. You may discover you have neither the drive nor the personal commitment to start your own business. Believe me, that is the number-one reason so many people fail. Failure always happens when people would rather hide behind justifications and excuses than to move on and change.

The second part of the Prosperity Equation discusses the specifics of selecting and starting a new business or growing and developing an existing business. In these chapters, I have attempted to speak from my personal experience, often referring to how I started and developed my own companies. It involves stories about the struggles and the victories I experienced as the companies grew. These chapters analyze those events that made the companies grow and prosper, as well as the mistakes, traps, and pitfalls I fell into along the way.

And finally, the last part of this book deals with some specifics of marketing, advertising, promoting, and selling your products or services. No matter how great your service or product is, you will be doomed to an early bankruptcy if you lack the expertise to sell and market your business. I have known many talented business people who had an aversion, even a disdain for sales. Even though they had a great product or service, sometimes actually a better product than their competition, their companies are now gone and they have returned to the workforce. Many times throughout history, a superior product has lost the sale to a superior presentation.

This book is not for everyone

If you are able to fully understand and apply the principles and philosophies I am about to share with you, your life will explode. Wonderful things are about to happen for you and your family. The information in this book is worth several hundred thousand times what you've paid for it. Sadly enough though, just to slap a little cold water in your face, the truth of the matter is most of you will never get it. Most people have been raised and conditioned all of their lives to fail. Statistically, the odds have been stacked up against you since birth. If you are like most people, you have never been given the tools to be a success in life.

What is Prosperity?

Although Prosperity involves wealth, money is only used to keep score. Money alone cannot buy happiness. The Bible tells us, "The love of money is the root of all evil." Read the words literally. It says "the love of money." When I think about those words, I think about Ebenezer Scrooge in Dickens' *A Christmas Carol.*

Scrooge amassed a fortune and lived a frugal, self-centered life. He loved his money and nothing else. Although he was a wealthy man, his soul wasn't liberated until he actually spent his money. In the end his money made a lot of other people happy. Of course, in the process of spending his money, old Scrooge himself received a great deal of pleasure because he experienced the good things his money made possible.

Money in and of itself has no value. Money becomes real only when you are spending it. That is one of the main reasons most of us are not able to save more money than we do. When you see a balance on your bank statement, it's just a bunch of numbers on a piece of paper. It only becomes real when you draw it out and buy something with it.

If you've ever spent any time in the gambling casinos in Las Vegas or Atlantic City, did you ever stop and wonder why they play with plastic chips instead of making bets with real cash? The basic psychology here is powerful. The players lose sight of the fact that the chips are actually real money. It's easier to lose plastic chips than to lose real money—or at least that's the illusion it creates in people's minds.

The world is teeming with people whose lives are overflowing with despair and misery, people whose destiny is dictated by their poverty. How could anyone in his or her right mind even begin to insinuate that a wealthy person doesn't have at least a better shot at living a happy fulfilled life? Poverty is not a virtue; it is a curse.

Since childhood you've been subjected to a parade of self-righteous losers, marching through your life programming your mind to fail. Everyone told you "money can't buy happiness" and unfortunately, many of us bought into that lie. Many people have filed that garbage somewhere deep into their subconscious mind. I have met people who actually felt guilty because they achieved success. It is all of this negative programming that holds many people back and keeps them from having the prosperity they deserve. Well, let me say this about that, all of the things in my life that make me happy and healthy are much more accessible to me because I have money. Having money creates choices and peace of mind. I am convinced that poor people have more stress and more worry in their lives than wealthy people.

Although money won't buy your good health, it certainly will make the finest physicians and the best quality medical services available to you. It will certainly give you the time, resources, and freedom to pursue your dreams and exercise your creativity.

You don't have to be a criminal to be prosperous—although that's certainly one of your options if that's the road you choose to take. But there are better ways to get there with a lot less risk involved. If you really understand the power of the Prosperity

Equation, there is never a need to lie or cheat or sneak or deceive to get what you want; you must, however, develop a business mind-set. You have to learn to be straightforward and direct in matters concerning business. Business decisions are rational and seldom emotional. You must be able to see things clearly, as they actually are.

Sometimes a business mind-set requires you to speak bluntly, with a type of brutal frankness you would never use in a social environment. Sometimes you have to make difficult business decisions. Some of these decisions may have an adverse effect on the lives of people you genuinely like. Sometimes you have to have the guts to say no when everyone else is urging you to go forward with a project that means a lot to them. All of these things go with the territory. Many wealthy businesspeople amassed their fortunes because they were calculated, aggressive, and intense by nature.

How rich is rich?

How much is enough? An important thing we need to take a look at is just how much do you have to have before you would consider yourself to be wealthy? Do you honestly think you have the time or the dedication it takes to become a billionaire? A billion dollars is an incredible amount of money. When you are talking about that kind of money, the odds are overwhelmingly stacked against you. Becoming a billionaire is an extreme long shot, highly improbable, but I believe virtually everyone reading this book does have the ability to become a millionaire in a relatively short amount of time.

I have never even taken a shot at those lofty levels of personal wealth of a Bill Gates or a Warren Buffet.

Enough is enough. The majority of people I meet in my seminars and in my day-to-day travels do not have Enough Money. There is a distinction between being Stupid Stinking Rich and having Enough Money. When people have Enough Money, they never have to ask how much something costs before they decide to buy it. You want to go to Europe next week? No problem!

Now, that's having Enough Money. One of the exercises in the Prosperity Seminars focuses on getting individuals in touch with the concept of just how much is enough.

There are literally millions of millionaires. There are probably several hundred millionaires living within just a few miles of your home. Most likely, you rub elbows with them every day at the supermarket or at the car wash. They go to your church and their kids play with yours. It just isn't that big a deal anymore. Frankly, in today's economy, a million dollars just ain't what it used to be. Even so, it is an awful lot of money. Although millionaires seem to have become rather prevalent in today's society, considering the fact you have chosen to buy this book, I am going to assume you are not one of them and you'd like to be.

Money is freedom

Prosperity involves the complete quality of your life. Living in a fine home and eating fine food, wearing fine clothes and jewelry, driving fine cars, traveling the world, and doing everything you've always wanted to do. That's only a fraction of it. Prosperity is having enough money to share your good fortune to help others. Prosperity is providing everything for your family and the people you care about. Prosperity is having freedom of choices and making your own decisions without limitations. Prosperity is about your spiritual peace of mind and your personal health. It's about not having to worry about the future.

When I attempt to explain how Prosperity creates freedom, many people have difficulty grasping the concept. What does wealth have to do with freedom? Well, it's sort of like this. It's when I can casually say to my wife, "Hey, how about us taking off this weekend? Let's take Zach [our son] and fly down to the Caymans?" That brand of spontaneous abandon is only possible to those who have achieved this level of affluence.

In one of my seminars, one of my students asked me a question: "Mr. Ziegler, why do you wear so much jewelry?"

My answer was short and simple and nonapologetic: "Because I can!"

The greatest single secret I learned in my quest for wealth and security was that most of the Prosperity Equation takes place in your head.

You'll never win until you accept responsibility for your own successes and failures

So many people are leading lives of desperation, stuck in jobs they hate, in relationships that aren't working. They don't have the guts to break out or to even attempt to make a change. My observation is that most people die while they are still waiting for the right moment to make their move. They never even got off of square one because they lacked self-confidence and conviction. Life is filled with people who refuse to throw away their insecurities and psychological security blankets.

It is a fact that most of the problems in most people's lives and relationships are, in the end, a result of their financial problems. Talking to people who are divorced, you'll find most of them will tell you the real underlying reason for the breakup of their marriage started out with financial problems. In truth, the lack of money is the root of most evils in our lives.

I believe most people spend their entire lives living in the past as if it were some sort of magical time. They wish they could get back there to some time in their past and live there forever. I wonder how many people live their entire lives in fear, wishing they could regress back to the security of their childhood.

You'll find those same people desperately looking forward to the future hoping they will stumble upon some kind of magic cure for everything that's wrong with their lives. Every Friday you see them lining up at the counters of their neighborhood convenience stores to buy their lottery tickets. They're only buying themselves a little hope, dreaming about instant wealth and prosperity with no personal investment. They drudge through their uneventful, day-by-day lives as if the present is something they must get through, one day at a time. The "right now" in their lives is just something to be endured until the good times return.

Rats in the maze

Recently, I stumbled across an incredible little book titled *Who Moved My Cheese? An Amazing Way to Deal with Change in Your Work and in Your Life* by Spencer Johnson, M.D. You may recall Johnson was the coauthor of *The One Minute Manager*.

I first saw the book, *Who Moved My Cheese?* as I was rushing through a concourse at O'Hare Airport in Chicago. The moment I saw the title I was paralyzed by a powerful flashback. My mind raced back through time as twenty-five-year-old memories bubbled to the surface.

I was sitting cross-legged on the carpeted floor of a hotel ballroom. My eyes were closed, eyelids lightly fluttering, both hands resting on my lap, both palms turned upward. This was a kinder, gentler, less worldly, twenty-seven-year-old Jim Ziegler. Here I was chanting my personal top-secret mantra over and over again. There were fifty other people scattered around the darkened room, each one chanting, all of them seeking a higher level of enlightenment.

For just a flicker of a moment in time, way back there in the seventies, I found myself searching for the hidden spiritual meanings of the universe, or something like that. Before I was thirty, I had already enjoyed a great career as a nationally known radio announcer and as a record-setting radio-advertising salesman. Now, here I was broke and divorced, confused, and angry. I was sitting in a hotel ballroom humming words that had no meaning.

Within the confines of a single frame in the motion pictures of my life, that was a special period of time. The entire episode lasted less than three years but shaped my destiny. During this period I dropped out completely and attended literally dozens of awareness seminars and self-discovery retreats. It was during this time in my life that I first heard the story about the rats in the maze.

Returning to the present and my current reality…It took less than an hour during the flight home to Atlanta to read the little book from cover to cover. What an incredible book! It was very close to the way I remembered the story, with several small variations. Reading it today had the same impact I experienced nearly thirty years before when I first heard it. Johnson told the tale of two rats and two little people who lived in a giant maze. They had designed their entire lives around what they thought was an unlimited supply of cheese. Of course, one day when they suddenly realized the cheese was gone, their lives were turned upside-down. The book is about how the four different personalities dealt with the catastrophic changes they had to face in their lives, how each one handled the quest for new cheese. Each of us needs to read this book cover to cover, several times. I recommend you give a copy to all of your friends and to every employee in your organization, and then conduct meetings to discuss what they got out of it.

Change is inevitable. It has always been with us. Even now as you sit here reading these words, everything around you is dying or being born. The universe is fluid and constantly in a state of flux. Nothing will ever stay the way it was.

In business, as in life, you cannot hang onto the way it used to be. What if the IBM Corporation had stubbornly continued to focus their corporate vision on the design and sale of typewriters? Of course, we all know IBM was once the undisputed world leader in typewriter sales. I still own an IBM Selectric III—I am sure I could locate it somewhere in the attic or a storage room if you really wanted to see it.

When IBM first realized the impact computer technology was going to have on our lives, IBM executives made a decision to change all of their old paradigms. They knew it was only a matter of time before computers would replace the typewriter with advanced word processing. IBM was right out there, on the front lines of change. Many people credit IBM with leading us into the personal computer age.

Thousands of industries have been forced to change or die. It's sort of like when compact discs replaced vinyl records. I don't believe I even know anyone who still owns a turntable. Where can you even buy phonograph needles? The record industry endured nearly a hundred years, but within the blink of an eye it was over. It wasn't a gradual transition. The entire revolution was over in less than three or four years and vinyl records were suddenly and completely obsolete. If the executives in those record companies hadn't been flexible or open to change, they would have resembled dinosaurs being sucked down into the tar pits, loudly protesting the inevitable.

Examples of your changing world are all around you every moment of your life. Think of all of the things that have changed in your life and in the lives of people you know.

Have you ever met someone who continues to wear hairstyles or fashions that went out of style ten or twenty years ago? What used to be cool now inspires ridicule.

Did you ever try to go back and visit the old neighborhood?

Have you ever tried to look up someone you knew a long time ago?

Maybe you've experienced the fumbling stabs at meaningful conversation with your old friends at a class reunion. Everyone and everything change with the passage of time.

No matter how hard you resist, the world keeps moving in new directions. You can choose to move with it—or even ahead of it—or you will be run over by it. There is one thing you can chisel in granite. No matter how hard you resist, you can never go back.

People are usually afraid and resistant to change. Of course, not all change is good, but the question you have to ask yourself is, "Is this change inevitable?" People who are stubborn, unwilling to adapt or react to inevitable change, are destined to lose. If it's an absolute certainty, go with it. People who ride the crest of the new wave will reach the beach first.

We all have our own personal paradigms, belief systems we use to measure our reality. Many times in my life, I have had to examine those very basic beliefs I had always held to be true. Creating new beliefs and new perceptions of reality is one of the most difficult tasks anyone ever has to face. Once you have made the conscious decision to change, it challenges the essence of who or what you thought you were.

18

Are you holding onto old obsolete personal paradigms? Do these beliefs limit your success? If you are hanging onto inflexible beliefs about the way things are, are those beliefs holding you back? Is it possible for you to move on without accepting change? I would never have achieved the success I currently enjoy if I had not made fundamental changes in my core beliefs. There was a lot of realization, sometimes painful, before I was able to move forward. Realization is the mother of actualization.

Your life is the result of the choices you've made

I have encountered so many people who tend to be whiners and excuse-makers. They've allowed their lives to become reduced to an endless series of petty, insignificant dramas that revolve around justification and blaming others instead of accepting responsibility for their own successes and failures. The world is teeming with petty, meanspirited little people and they're all out to get you. They're infected with jealousy and envy. I am talking about those small thinkers who see giant problems in every tiny nonevent that makes up the fabric of their insignificant, meaningless, small existence.

Your life is the result of a series of choices you have made. You are wherever you are in your life, at whatever point you've arrived, at whatever levels of success and prosperity you are now enjoying because of the choices in life you have made. In truth, whether you wish to believe it or not, you are exactly what and where you have chosen to be. If you are not winning, or worse yet, if you are losing, it's because you have chosen to lose. If you are not particularly happy about the way things are, the answer should be obvious. Choose not to lose! Choose to win!

Stop whining

I've been knocked down hard, many times. Getting up and not giving up was always my only option. I never whine. Nobody wants to listen to it anyway. Nobody hangs with whiners except other whiners.

If your life has become reduced to a series of insignificant incidents that are constantly blown out of proportion, you'll never get the big picture. If you are ever really going to have all of those things you say you really want out of life, it is important to first get your mind right. I am talking about right now, immediately! One of the cornerstone pillars of success is your ability to achieve a focus in your life.

Life's losers do not have the ability to prioritize which things in life and business are truly important. We've all met those people whose priorities are completely out of order. They'll spend countless wasted hours obsessing about unimportant things, insignificant molehills, until these things become mountains and kill their spirits. If what you were extremely upset about yesterday cannot even be remembered today, then it was probably never important in the first place. Don't drain your energy obsessing about meaningless trivia. You will never be prosperous if you cannot eliminate all of those petty, insignificant intrigues from your life.

The decision

If you are ever going to have prosperity, you must first make a conscious decision to become a success. I can say that with absolute authority. The decision itself is multifaceted and requires many smaller decisions. As we have discussed, one of the first decisions you must face is to eliminate all negative, petty trivia from your life and concentrate on those things that really matter and the goals at hand. You are going to have to strip away any excuses you might be hiding behind, anything that might be a crutch, and anything that might hold you back. You can never be a success if you believe there are barriers between you and the goal. Winners have intensity and their mission is clearly defined. You must make a decision to achieve focus.

Why most people are destined to be employees

Let me see if I've got this right. You bought this book because you're thinking about starting your own business. You're dreaming about the day when you can step out there on your own. Looking forward to the day when you tell off the boss, clean out your desk, quit your job and never look back. Does that about sum it up?

If you wish to duplicate my success, let's start by taking a strong look at yourself. Do you have the drive and desire to succeed? Don't be too quick to answer. Actions are always louder than words. Success takes personal commitment, motivation, intensity, and the ability to hang in there.

We've all heard the statistics about new business failures. The reason the majority of new startup businesses wind up in bankruptcy is because the people who started them never mastered the basics. They weren't emotionally prepared for what they were getting into. Let's face the facts: the majority of people who work for someone else haven't got what it takes to do what it takes to step out there and become an entrepreneur. Most people are destined to be employees, not owners.

It's incredible how many people tell me they hate their jobs but they're not doing anything about it. Look around and ask yourself this question: "Will I ever get rich doing this?" Very few prosperous people are employees. If you're dissatisfied with the amount of money you are being paid, chances are you are probably being paid more than you are worth. Sorry, but it's absolutely true. Your relationship with your employer is supposed to be a value-for-value relationship. Is your employer really getting enough value out of your productivity to even justify your continued employment? Just because you show up every day and have been there a long time, does that justify a raise?

In my Prosperity Seminars, we have several exercises where we attempt to get the people attending the seminars to get in touch with the concept I call Your Personal, Marketable Value. This concept is an exercise where participants are asked to describe exactly what they are worth from a money standpoint. What is the value of your skill and knowledge to your employer or the consumers of your goods and services?

Okay, you've cleared the last couple of hurdles I threw at you and you still think you'd like to give it a try. You still want to be your own boss, right?

Maybe you're planning to start one of these fabulous home-based businesses. You're going to set your own hours. Work when you want to. Take off whenever you feel like it. You're going to be sitting around the house all day in your underwear making big bucks with your personal computer, telephone, and fax machine. Every day your mailbox is going to be stuffed with checks. You've read thousands of articles about it. It's easy! Millions of people have done it. Right?

Reality check! Earth to dreamer! Statistically, the chances are you'll never even get off the ground. Most people are all talk, pipe-dreamers with no real substance to their plans. If you're like most people at this stage in the process, you don't even have a written and clearly defined goal. There you are just flapping in the wind, hanging onto some flimsy pipe dream. It takes a lot of nerve to jump out here in Entrepreneurland and start a business on your own. As of yet, you haven't proved to yourself or to anybody else whether or not you've got what it takes. If you're getting angry now, remember this: I am just holding up a mirror here. If you don't like what you are seeing, are you honestly willing to do what it takes to change it? This is a real book for real entrepreneurs with the guts to go for it.

I want everything

If you really knew my history, the reasons I am successful would become obvious to you. I grew up in a rough, lower middle-class neighborhood and obtained only a high school education. I was one of three children, the son of an enlisted man in the U.S. Navy. Continuously employed since I was fourteen years old, I have held down two or three jobs at the same time for most of my life. Early on, I realized, if I was ever going to have anything in this world, I'd have to work hard, and go out there and get it for myself.

When I became an adult, I wanted expensive new cars and a big beautiful home in an upscale neighborhood. I wanted financial security and the freedom to make my own decisions. I wanted to be able to eat in the best restaurants and wear nice, name-brand clothes and fine jewelry, and to be able to provide the best for my family. I wanted luxury vacations and first-class travel, security, and a comfortable cushion to fall back on if I ever needed it. I wanted to have and experience it all. Desire is one of the cornerstone pillars of the Equation. Saying you would like to have these things is not enough. Are you willing to pay the price and invest in yourself? Today I have all of those things and much more.

> "I am where I am in my life because I am willing to do those things other people are not willing to do to get what they say they want."

I sincerely believe the majority of people on Earth are just trying to get to the end of their lives with their bills paid. They are not aiming at the higher levels of success or prosperity; they are just working and hoping they can make enough money to cover their financial nut each month. Few people are really ready to change until some external force pushes them out of their comfortable zones.

It takes guts to get out of a rut

You can't hit a home run if you never swing at the pitch. Don't come around whining and complaining because you hate your job and you're not getting those things out of life you'd really like to have. If you're stuck in a rut but you still haven't mustered up the nerve to take the risks and chances success demands, then you deserve not to have all of those things you don't have…nor everything you're never going to get. I have no sympathy for anyone who won't at least go for it.

I would hate to know I'd struck out in my life while I was standing there at the plate, never taking a swing at it, watching the pitches go by.

> "I would hate to know that I'd struck out in life looking at the pitches."

A story about my dad

His name was James Edward Ziegler but we always called him Chief. After thirty-four years of service to his country, thirteen cruises, and four wars, we buried Chief in his uniform back in May 1991. Dad was a big guy, a tough man, standing six-foot-three with a commanding presence and an electric intensity. He was a true leader.

As I write these words, there is a portrait of my father on the wall here in my office. I am looking at him wearing his dress uniform with eight gold stripes on his sleeve and two rows of medals and ribbons.

Chief only had an eighth grade education but he was one of the most brilliant men I have ever known. He read voraciously and was conversational in many deep, intellectual subjects. He inspired me to learn.

Even though we didn't have a lot of money, we were rich in many other ways. Chief was an honest and honorable man and he taught us morals and strong values, the meaning of right and wrong. I have to admit, I've lost my way numerous times, but no matter how far off-track I strayed, remembering Chief's values always brought me back to dead center.

One of the proudest moments in my old man's life was when I was awarded Eagle Scout. I can still see him sitting in the audience and smiling as I stood on the stage with the others and raised my right hand in the scout sign and said those words, "On my honor..." Few people today have the guts and conviction to stand up for anything they believe in. You will never become wealthy and successful if your word is worthless.

I really loved my father. In the last conversation we had before he died, he told me there were so many things he wished he had done. He looked at me through tear-filled eyes as he told me about all of those things he had always wanted to do and see and accomplish. It really shook me up when I realized he had sacrificed his dreams until it was too late.

It was the end of an era in my life when Chief passed away. To this day those values he taught me are still ingrained. The greatest lesson of all was the last one he ever taught me: You've got to go for it. Don't get all of the way to end of your life and find yourself regretting the choices you made. Don't die wishing you'd done it differently. I will die still reaching for that ever-elusive next level.

I have burned all of my bridges

Do you have a strong enough belief in yourself to take the leap of faith required to become a success in your own business? When I reached that point in my life, there was never a moment of doubt. It was never a gamble. I simply believed in myself.

Starting your own business requires intensity. Remembering back when I started my first company, there was a lot of adrenaline pumping. Clearly focused on my goal and totally committed to succeeding, there was never a thought of chickening out or turning back.

Now let me warn you, before you go stepping off the edge of that cliff, maybe you should stop and think about it one last time. Becoming an entrepreneur requires a risk-taker mentality. If you haven't got a sense of adventure, trust me, this isn't in the cards for you. Now is the time for a no-turning-back, teeth-clenched, eyes-blazing commitment. You've got to have discipline and a strong work ethic to get you where you say you want to be. Are you honestly prepared to work all of the hours and to do everything it takes to succeed?

You see, to become an independent businessman or businesswoman, you've got to put it all on the line. There's no sticking your toe in the water to see if you like it and there's no turning back.

Entrepreneur is a word derived from the French. It roughly translates as *opportunity taker*. An entrepreneur is a person who is not afraid to seize the moment, make the decision, and then follow through with it.

Have you got the guts to burn all of your bridges, right now, before you start? You'll never be prosperous if you are not willing to take substantial calculated risks in life. I have known too many people who thought they could start a business part-time to see whether or not they liked it. Maybe that's worked for someone, somewhere, but I never saw it. If that's your strategy, I think you're clinging to your insecurities and planning to fail.

Life is just a bucket of crabs

Success starts in the head. Your attitude is your most precious asset. Protect it at all costs. When you are planning to elevate yourself in any way, there are always going to be those people who will try to destroy your attitude.

When I was growing up in Jacksonville, Florida, I spent a lot of time playing around the banks of the St. Johns River. One of the happier memories of my childhood was when our whole family would go down under the Ortega River Bridge and fish for crabs.

Mom and Dad had both grown up in Baltimore, Maryland, and we really appreciated steaming up six or seven dozen blue crabs, Maryland style. That's an ingrained part of my family heritage. We'd all just sit around the table, which was all covered with newspaper, and then the five of us, along with two or three assorted neighbors, would go through a three-foot pile of steamed crabs. It usually took about an hour.

If you've ever fished for crabs, there is an old fisherman's adage that says, "If you put a crab in a bucket, you must put a lid on the bucket because it will climb out; but if you put two crabs in the bucket, there is no need

> to put a lid on it because neither crab will
> allow the other one to escape. They will cling
> to each other and they will continually pull
> each other back down."

I've caught thousands of crabs in my lifetime. It's the truth. Crabs in a bucket will latch onto each other and continually pull each other back down into the bucket, and will never allow each other to escape.

There are going to be many people who hate your success and will do or say anything and everything possible to pull you back down. Although they, themselves, have no desire to be successful, they don't want you to break out. If they see you have a positive attitude, these crabs will latch onto you and try to drag you back down to their level. They will be the first to tell you why you are going to fail, why it won't work, and why you shouldn't try it. They know for a fact the whole world is against them and it's always somebody else's fault.

I suspect more than a third of the people on the planet are the crabs in life. They've been dragging society down since biblical times. Crabs are pitiful, meanspirited little people who are always whispering negatives in your ear, trying to pull you back down.

The crabs of this world have a deeply ingrained welfare mentality. They are spiteful and envious. They expect their government, their employer, and their community to take care of them from cradle to grave. In their hearts they believe you owe them something. They are always looking for some way to get around the system and to get somebody else to pay their way. Crabs invented the concept of the free ride.

If I had listened to Mom and Dad, I would still be a welder on the night shift

Don't be infected or sidetracked by other people's insecurity. Sometimes people who genuinely love you and care about you will accidentally pull you down. Mom and Chief were working-class people with limited educations. They grew up during the Great Depression era. As a result, they were always cautious and traditional. You really couldn't expect them to understand my desire to be my own boss or my penchant for taking risks. They lived their entire lives looking forward to their own retirement. Mom and Dad always played it safe.

They finally persuaded me to get a civil service job. I became an apprentice sheet metal mechanic. The job had great benefits, good hourly pay, and a U.S. government retirement package. A government job was my parents' idea of the ultimate career.

I despised what I was doing. Even though the money was great, it was like being in prison. Just getting up and going to work every day was drudgery. One night, somewhere around ten o'clock, I walked up to the supervisor and turned in my name badge and my toolbox and walked off the job forever. Of course, my parents didn't understand. They were very disappointed.

My real love was my part-time job on the weekends as a rock-and-roll disk jockey. I found the broadcasting business glamorous and exciting. When I went full-time in the radio business, I learned about advertising and promotions. These skills would help me to achieve my goals later in life. For the first time in my life I was being paid for my talent and my creativity instead of my physical skills and labor. It had always been my dream to be paid more for what I knew than for what I was doing with my hands.

Later on, when I became a radio advertising salesman, I studied and perfected the fine points of my trade. I was rapidly learning what it meant to be a professional salesman. By this time I was already making more money than I could ever to have hoped to make as a welder.

If I had listened to Mom and Dad—if I had never taken any chances—I would probably still be a welder on the night shift.

The real story here is how my experiences in the broadcasting industry built the foundations for the successes I am experiencing today. What I learned about advertising and promotions in those early years, way back then, helped get me to the point where I am today. Looking back on those early days when I first broke into full-time professional sales, I can truthfully say I was paying my dues experientially.

Later on, as the Prosperity Equation unfolds, I will discuss how to start and select a specific business. Look at your entire life as a learning curve made up of a collection of interrelated experiences. Your Personal, Marketable Value is expanded by the quality of your experiences.

Everything you've read so far is designed to shake you up and show you there is nothing beyond your reach. I am attempting to get you to think, dream, and focus on your future. I am talking about your future as it can be. In order to realistically map out a course of action, we need to stop and take your personal inventory. It is important for you to become aware of the unique cash value of your past personal experiences. Everything you've ever done in your life has a marketable significance you can capitalize on. All of the experiential hardships you are enduring today have future value.

Life is no more than a collection of your personal experiences. The adventures I have lived in my life represent an investment I made years ago that is paying off today. Your life and everything you have learned from your experiences, good or bad, have a collateral value you can put in the bank today.

Leverage other people's experience

This is another one of those essential elements of the Prosperity Equation. How many times have you ever heard an older person say the following words? "If only I knew then what I know now, I would be a millionaire!" Unfortunately, that's painfully true. Life plays many cruel jokes on most of us. By the time you are finally able to figure it all out by yourself, it's too late. There just isn't enough time for most people to get there and enjoy it before the final curtain falls on their lives.

Could you imagine where you would be if you had to invent simple math or the written word all by yourself? I am glad someone invented the automobile before I was born so I didn't have to waste years of my life trying to figure it out. In other words, to become a success you have to leverage other people's knowledge. When you flick on a light switch, you are using an invention that is the result of someone else's knowledge. Do you have the expertise to make your own lightbulb from scratch? If you were marooned on a desert island, could you make a lightbulb from raw materials? Of course not! If you did, then you'd have to manufacture electricity, and so on, and so on. We leverage the knowledge and the production of other people in society for the greater good of everyone.

Another one of the essential elements of the Prosperity Equation is to surround yourself with successful people. You should seek out those who know what you don't know and can do what you haven't learned to do. Absorb the knowledge of others who have been there before you. Hire people who have skills and knowledge you lack.

Saturate your mind with success

To be truly prosperous, you must leverage other people's experience if you intend to ever get ahead of the curve. Early on, I made the commitment to Saturate My Mind With Success, another essential ingredient for Prosperity. Later on, I will describe exactly how I discovered this important concept when I first began building the framework to assemble my fortune.

> "You are the result of everything that you have ever experienced and that point to which it has brought you."
>
> —*Dr. Frederick S. Perls, circa 1970*

As a consultant, professional speaker, and author, the only value I have to those people who pay for my services is my ability to give them the benefits of all of the things I have experienced over the course of my life and career. The reason you paid for this book is because I am sharing the techniques and secrets of my success. You are paying for the meat and the substance of what I have done and seen and touched in my life. You are not paying for some theories I learned in school but never experienced in real life.

 "Education is not a credential, it is only a qualification."

Throughout this book, there will be a number of times when I will take the liberty of quoting myself when I think something I said is original and significant. Usually, when I do this, these are signature statements taken from my seminars.

So many people rely on their educational credentials as if their degree guarantees them success in life. *Your education is not a credential; it is only a qualification.* Experience is the only true and valid credential.

Perhaps you've heard the expression "thinking outside of the box"? For many people, their advanced educations have become the curse of their lives. So many people don't have the ability to create anything original because their schooling taught them conformity and rigid thinking. Their education has taken away their ability to go outside of the box. Our business schools today are turning out armies of middle managers with advanced, cookie-cutter educations, when in truth, most wealthy and prosperous people are free-spirited entrepreneurs with limited formal educations. I have met many frustrated PhDs who never achieve wealth because they have no real life, no real world experience.(Have you heard the joke that PhD means Pizza Hut delivery?)

If you really want to impress me, tell me about the events, the skills, and the experiential knowledge you've gathered in your life. I judge the value of a person by their character and their personal experiences. Don't whine to me about why life isn't fair because you've got this advanced degree and you're still not getting any cheese.

31

A *welfare mentality*

You're not getting all of those things you want out of life? So what! The world doesn't owe you a living, much less prosperity. The United States of America only guarantees life, liberty, and the pursuit of happiness. Happiness is not a constitutional right; you only have the right to be allowed to go for it. Nobody owes you happiness or success. And if you are a failure, it's neither my fault nor my responsibility. Don't stack your baggage on my doorstep. If you're not happy or prosperous, whose fault is it anyway? I will never allow you to pawn off any of your guilt on me. How can anyone expect to ever become prosperous if they refuse to take charge of their own lives?

Roadkill is strewn across life's highway! Yes, The highways of our lives are filled with the flattened carcasses of wimps and whiners and other varieties of assorted losers who will envy your successes and automatically assume they have a right to what you have legitimately earned. Remember, you have a right to be successful and prosperous. The crabs are always going to take potshots at you. They don't want to succeed or to better themselves. It is the sole purpose and the primary mission of their lives to drag you back down to their level. Misery loves company.

Life ain't fair and so what

Many people have manufactured excuses about why it is okay to fail because life dealt them a bad hand. It's incredible that so many people feel it is impossible for them to succeed because there are factors in life they perceive to be beyond their control.

Yes, there is discrimination in the world. Injustice. And it's wrong. There are many people out there filled with hate and jealousy. But that is no excuse for self-pity. You will only lose if you choose not to go for it.

There are many people out there who desperately need our help. All children deserve a head start. They need the education and the emotional tools to break out and succeed. That's not what I am talking about here. I am talking directly about and directly to those people who believe they have a right to give up and lie down because they think life isn't fair.

I believe some people actually take comfort in the idea that factors beyond their control are causing them to be stuck at the bottom of every pile and the end of every line. I am sick of catering to life's whiners and professional victims. It appears as if some people might actually enjoy whining more than winning.

Dr. Frederick S. Perls said something at a self-awareness seminar back in the seventies: "What is…is…and what ain't…ain't…and so what!"

I have always called this particular Perls quote the theory of reality. You can't change "what is" by wishing that "it wasn't." Things are the way they are. Change only takes place in the future not in the present. End of discussion!

Why would anyone want to go through life hiding behind some built-in excuse why their life isn't working? What is the point of someone justifying all of their failures and nonaccomplishments with the pride of knowing it's not their fault? If this sounds familiar, stop blaming your problems and failures on other people and what is beyond your control. One thing prosperous people have in common is they've taken charge of their lives. No excuses!

Successful people must be prepared to be disliked

In the book *Think and Grow Rich*, Napoleon Hill lists the fear of criticism as one of the biggest single reasons many people do not achieve wealth and prosperity. Looking back through my personal experiences over the course of my entire life, I have found this to be true. With most of us, it started when you were a teenager and peer pressure began to control your life. You can probably remember doing some incredibly stupid things to be accepted by the other kids. You didn't want to be criticized. That mentality spilled over into our adult lives and, subconsciously, it still tries to hold us back.

One of the common characteristics shared by most of the world's wealthiest and most successful people is that they are different from other people. The quickest route to failure is to conform and do what everyone else is doing. This should be obvious. If you want to become wealthy, you've got to do things differently.

A person who is operating with a winning mind-set must be able to go with his or her gut instinct. Once you become totally tuned-in, you'll make decisions quickly and, usually, accurately. People who are not used to operating on that level will call you impulsive. I have limited patience with slow thinkers and indecisive people.

You must be prepared to do the right thing even if it is unpopular.

Have no envy

I don't want what you have and I will waste no energy trying to bring you down. There's no time in my life for those petty intrigues and jealousies. I genuinely want you to be the ultimate success. Nothing would please me more than if you were to read this book and become tremendously wealthy as a result. I will be extremely happy if your achievements in life surpass mine.

I thrill in other people's successes. Over the last decade I have legitimately helped many people get started. I will celebrate your success and I will be enthusiastically happy for you when you have it. I am your greatest cheerleader!

Celebrate the achievements of others. Support them. Don't envy the winners in life or resent them for it. It is ironic when you pause and realize almost everyone would love to be rich. If the pursuit of happiness is an American dream, why do so many people dedicate so much energy attacking wealthy people as if we've done something wrong? Our politicians have a field day with their Tax the Wealthy platforms. Religious zealots try to make you feel guilty for having it. At the same time, they are trying to pick your pocket.

If you ever catch yourself taking shots at the wealthy, remember they are only doing what you would love to be able to do. If life is truly a bucket of crabs, don't be one of them. You will never reach any level of personal prosperity if you are constantly pulling other people down; it kills your positive energy.

See each person as an individual

I have had to change many things about myself in my quest for success. Prejudice and intolerance are major roadblocks on the road to riches. When I learned to see each person as an individual, it resulted in one of the most important revelations of my life. It is an essential element in the Equation.

We live in a diverse world, and, whether you like it like it not, you have to be able to interact with a broad variety of people of different races, religions, and nationalities. This was really hard for me. Growing up, I had developed an extensive, long laundry list of exactly what type of people I didn't like.

This was one of my most difficult challenges. It was a major mind-shift for me when I made a conscious decision to evaluate each individual I meet on his or her own personal qualities and values instead of seeing them as part of a larger group. Sometimes when I am making a judgmental decision about someone, I just look at them and think to myself, "They're just doing the best they can." Everyone is just trying to be happy, and I can't begrudge him or her the opportunity to go for it. I have learned to celebrate other people's victories and to reach out to them.

Now, don't get me wrong. There are losers in every group, every race, every religion, and every nationality. I still reserve the right to dislike people who have criminal values. I still have no use for wimps and whiners and losers of any description, no matter what their race, nationality, or religion happens to be. It usually makes me angry when people are clannish. If people of a particular religion or group exclude me as a person, I have a problem with that. Most of us have a tendency to dislike people who dislike us. In other words, I have learned to despise racists, no matter what race they happen to belong to themselves. My desire for tolerance is all about genuinely giving everyone a chance as an individual, instead of blindly categorizing him or her by stereotype as part of a group.

Prejudice is destructive. It holds you back and limits your opportunities. Many of the people who knew me thirty years ago are still solidly stuck in their old paradigms. They are actually amazed to find out I have friends from foreign countries, other races, and other cultures. I have developed friendships and business relationships with all types of people.

If your personal paradigm involves intolerance, you will never be able to advance to the highest levels of the Prosperity Equation. You must open your mind and make a sincere commitment to understand where other people are coming from and to see their point of view. Until you are able to crash through all of your personal barriers, you will never be able to move on to the greater levels of success. Dedicate all of your energy toward positive goals without barriers and distractions.

The bottom line is all about the bottom line. In today's world chances are you will never be prosperous and successful if you have built walls between you and other people. Reach out and embrace diversity and you will find out "those people" are really not much different from you.

Get out of my way!

I sincerely hope everyone in the world gets everything he or she wants out of his or her lives. I really want your life to turn out exactly the way you want it to be. My sincere and heartfelt desire is for you to have everything you have ever wished for. I wish you the absolute best, no matter who you are. As long as you stay out of my way! I have many personal friends who fall into some of the categories and mentalities I'm describing in this book. There's nothing wrong with anyone choosing to be any way they want to be as long as they respect my right not to be like them.

I get up every morning feeling alive and free. I am totally in charge of my destiny. Let me be who I am and in return, I will respect your dreams and your lifestyle.

Clinging to that retirement dream

Right now, I want you to stop, put this book down, go out and pick up this morning's newspaper, and turn to the business section. Some major corporation, somewhere, just announced plans to lay off hundreds or even thousands of people, right? Turn on the television at six o'clock. Read *Businessweek* magazine or *Time* or *Newsweek*. No matter what year it is, no matter what day it is, the news is the same. The one thing most of those laid-off people have in common is that they trusted and depended on their company and their government to take care of them. They have what I describe as "retirement mentality."

Laid off, downsized, and discarded

One of the greatest human tragedies has to be a laid-off executive who relied on his/her education and the years they had invested with the company to get them through all of the way to the end of their life. Now they find themselves downsized and discarded, bitter, out of work, laid off, middle-aged, and starting over. Corporations throw away people as if they were discarding an old dishrag.

My father gave thirty-four years of his life to the U.S. Navy in return for promises and covenants made to him by the U.S. government. In his last years he saw those promises broken as Congress chipped away at his earned retirement benefits.

The Generation X employee, those people in their twenties and thirties here at the dawn of the millennium, will likely experience multiple job changes over the course of a lifetime. In the modern workforce, neither the employees nor the employers view their employment contract as a lifelong relationship. For most of the people out there who are still running in the twenty-first century rat race, it's going to be a bumpy ride. You must take control of your destiny. Even if you are young and optimistic, chances are the retirement income you were counting on will probably never materialize. That is why it makes so much sense for younger people to grab hold of their own destiny and start planning their own business.

We've seen our corporations and our government continuing to export the best jobs to foreign countries. Young people today are faced with dwindling opportunities in the job market. Once again, the choices appear to be obvious, you can either start your own, highly profitable business or learn to super-size fries.

I recently read an article predicting a record 1.4 million Americans will declare personal bankruptcy in this coming year. It is a fact that the individual standard of living in the United States is separating our society into two classes. The middle class is rapidly disappearing.

There's no security

There are no guarantees in life. Don't count on Social Security. It probably won't be there for you. The politicians have gutted the Social Security fund. They have borrowed trillions against your money to fund other programs.

I am a fifty-four-year-old man, a Baby Boomer. Well, guess what, folks. My generation is about to wake up to the realization that most of us are totally screwed. There isn't enough money to retire and the government will not be able to support you. I envision many of my lifelong friends living out their final years in poverty.

People looking for security and guaranteed retirement in today's world will probably suffer major disappointments in their lives. Many of them will go to their graves broke and bitter, still blaming their company and their government for not taking better care of them. But truthfully, it is their own fault because they never grabbed the wheel and took control of steering their own destiny.

Me retire? Never!

People often ask me, "What do you like to do for fun?"

I always answer, "Everything!"

I have no plans to retire. Heck, I'm having too much fun. The very idea of retirement horrifies me. What a repulsive concept. I already have a gold watch; if I really wanted another one, I'd just go out and buy one, or two, or three, or four.

My dream is to die on the speaker's podium during a wild standing ovation from four thousand cheering people directly after I performed the most magnificent speech of my entire career. I'll be standing up there on the speaker's platform, smiling, taking bows, waving, soaking up the applause, and then suddenly a weird look will appear on my face. I will grab my chest, then thud! Curtains. The end.

Retirement is only a goal for those people who hate their work. People who genuinely love what they do would never want to retire. I prefer to die working, vibrant and alive, than to die miserable, sitting around waiting for death. One thing you can be sure of is that I will be alive until the very moment I die.

If you've got a retirement mentality, starting your own business is probably a bad idea anyway. You're going to have a heart attack or a nervous breakdown or something like that. Don't do it! This isn't for you. Relax, put the book down, and go fishing or something.

It all boils down to your priorities. Some of us are destined to grab the golden ring while others are destined to play shuffleboard. I intend to die while I am still making a significant difference. At the same time, there are others who may be content to retire and get a part-time job handing out the carts at Wal-Mart. If that's all you want, then I suppose that's a beautiful thing too.

Vacation mentality

Have you been infected with the disease I call the vacation mentality?

If you live to play, if you're always planning for your next vacation, forget it! That is an employee mentality, not a business owner's mind-set. Entrepreneurs are driven.

Vacation-mentality people are always looking for a day off and they can hardly wait for five o'clock to roll around. They are still lobbying for the four-day workweek. Every Friday by two o'clock, they're already down the road off for the weekend. Vacation-mentality people always show up late and leave early.

It never ceases to amaze me when I am interviewing a prospective employee to work for me just how many people have no drive whatsoever. I immediately eliminate those applicants when they inquire about how much time off they are going to get before they ask questions about the position or the money or the advancement opportunities.

> "Those people who are always telling you to stop and smell the roses probably can't afford to buy any damn roses."

Have you ever noticed, the majority of people lecturing you that "money isn't everything," don't have any? The crabs in life have one goal, and that is to drag you down to their level so they can justify to themselves their own lack of success. The majority of people who put down wealth don't have it, never will have it, and are incapable of ever attaining it.

What motivates you?

As a manager, then as a business owner, author, and public speaker, I have had the opportunity to observe many people in their less-guarded moments. If you are preparing to start a business of your own, do you have the courage to examine your motives?

Many people start a business because they think it's going to be a cakewalk. Believe me, whatever you are doing right now is probably a lot easier than starting and running your own company.

Many businesses fail because these new entrepreneurs were not mentally or emotionally prepared for the uncertainty and insecurity that go with the territory. The first bump in the road was devastating. They weren't prepared, they didn't have the right temperament, and they went into it for all of the wrong reasons to begin with.

40

Owning your own business and being your own boss is not for everyone. It takes a certain type of person. Regardless of whether you buy into my observations about this or not, this chapter should be insightful when you are dealing with others. Through the years of interacting with my fellow human beings in assorted situations and circumstances, I have developed the nasty habit of categorizing everyone I meet. After I have gotten to know them, I can usually categorize just about everyone's personality into to one of these niches.

As a professional business consultant, I have developed a reputation among my clients for being a Quick Read. What this means is that I can literally walk through someone's company, talk to a few employees, look at a few situations, ask a couple of questions and then turn around and immediately suggest dramatic changes in the way they do business. I am paid an incredible amount of money because I possess this talent.

People spend their entire lives portraying themselves to others as if they were actors in a stage play. They assume the role in life of whom they think they are and who they think they are supposed to be. Sometimes the other supporting actors in their lives convince them their character is doomed to fail in life. So they write it into the script and make sure they live their lives in such a way as to fit the fate of the character they have created for themselves.

Read the following personality categories with a fully open mind and see if you can spot yourself and some of the other supporting actors in your life.

Money-motivated people

Money-motivated people are life's bottom feeders. They've got no character, no sense of honor, no depth, and no loyalty. They lack ethics and moral values. These people make excellent hookers, pawnbrokers, and loan sharks. You can never trust a person who is truly money motivated.

Are you money motivated? I certainly hope not. In my experience, money-motivated people are life's losers. I've often heard sales managers say they wish they could hire more sales representatives who are more money motivated. Of course, they don't really mean money motivated. In fact, they should be looking for achievement-oriented people.

To me, money is just one of the ways life's winners keep score.

Recognition-motivated people

My Labrador retriever, Buffy, is recognition motivated. Give her a pat on the head, rub her stomach, give her a few bones, and she's happy. Recognition-motivated people are the opposite of money-motivated people. They would prefer a title on their business card or a management promotion instead of a financial reward. Recognition-motivated people prefer a pat on the back, public applause, and an honorable mention in the newspaper. They make great volunteers.

Most recognition-motivated people began their quest for acceptance back in elementary school when they first volunteered to become hall monitors. Recognition-motivated people also rate very low on my respect meter.

Everyone needs some recognition for his or her accomplishments and achievements. Successful and prosperous people need positive feedback. Recognition-motivated people are stuffed-shirt personalities who believe their title alone makes him or her out to be somebody important.

Leadership-motivated people

Leadership-motivated people are close relatives of the recognition-motivated wimp I described in the previous paragraph.

If you are truly leadership motivated, all you need to be completely happy is to be in charge. The most notable example of a leadership-motivated personality that immediately springs to mind is Deputy Barney Fife from *The Andy Griffith Show.*

Creativity-motivated people

Of course, you might be one of those artsy-craftsy folks. Maybe you're one of those Birkenstocks-wearing intellectuals. Many people choose to be creativity motivated.

There is clearly a need in this world for the artists and the entertainers. It's perfectly wonderful if this is the way they have chosen to live their lives. I am only pointing out the obvious. They rarely make good business people. It's something about which side of the brain their life operates out of. Anyway, I don't have anything against them and many of them do become wealthy. They just don't fit into the entrepreneurial profile described in this forum.

Of course, many people are philosophic, idealistic, and artistic. They will be the first to tell you there are more important things in life than money and success and all of those things I live and breathe every day of my life.

Maybe you are prepared to sacrifice your whole life for a cause or an organization or a charity. Well, God bless you. I would never put you down for dedicating your life to a noble cause. But, if that's where you're coming from, allow me to ask you a question: Why in the hell did you buy this book?

As a footnote here, it has also been my experience that martyrs don't usually fit into the entrepreneurial profile either.

Success-motivated people

Perhaps you are one of those rare success-motivated individuals who have the drive, the ambition, and the talent to succeed. A strong work ethic is essential. There is no vacation mentality spoken here.

Success-motivated people will have all of the money, all of the recognition, and all of the quality time all of those other shallow, frustrated personalities can only dream about. Success-motivated people are the real leaders because they have to be extremely creative to achieve. Success-motivated people are naturally charitable and giving. They are always reaching out and helping others to achieve. Success-motivated people have strong ethics and morals, ideals and loyalty. They have no time to become ensnared in petty intrigues and other insignificant distractions in their lives. They are totally focused on their goals and principles. And as you may have already guessed, success-motivated people are the leaders, looked up to and recognized by others. They're artistic and imaginative.

The real winners in life are sensitive and caring about those who have less. Poverty is not a virtue. Being poor is not noble. The best way to help the poor is not by supporting them for the rest of their lives or by becoming one of them. Please don't misinterpret what I am trying to say here. I am not putting down poor people. I do have compassion and charity in my heart. I clearly make a distinction in my mind and I am always ready to help those who truly are in need.

Competition-motivated people

Successful people are competitive by nature. Every morning I look in the mirror, I remind myself that "today I am going to win."

Man's—and woman's—competitive nature is a fundamental human instinct. It's a basic survival need. Close your eyes for just a moment and picture Earth several million years ago. A caveman wakes up at the first light of dawn. He looks down at his family still sleeping near the smoldering ashes of last night's fire. He slings his heavy club over his shoulder and walks out of the cave to meet the rising sun with these words on lips: "Today I am going to kill something!"

Of course that was way back then at a time when man really was a hunter—a time when the animals actually did have a sporting chance. The caveman had to be faster and smarter than his prey and there was always the risk that he would end up becoming "prey" himself. There was also the possibility that he would come home with nothing and his family would not eat. Cavemen and cavewomen were entrepreneurs out of necessity. We have strong evidence that early man bartered and traded. We know they were forced to be at the top of their game every day just to survive. They were in competition with nature and the elements as well as other tribes. From birth they were taught to live in a hostile, competitive world.

My opinion of the public school system, to which we entrust our children in today's highly competitive world, is admittedly negative. I feel our young people are being systematically deprogrammed. Our institutions are training them to become just another ant on the anthill. The system is injecting our children with ever-larger doses of conformity, systematically assassinating these beautiful, young, competitive spirits.

Of course there are many wonderful, professional teachers out there who really do care. Were it not for the patience and the dedication of some really great teachers, I would not be able to express these thoughts on paper today.

When we talk about "thinking outside of the box," I submit to you that our schools are "the box." Despite the fact that many schoolteachers are dedicated and professional, there are even more who are inept, apathetic, and unqualified. And the school system supports them.

When children are born, they are fearless. They assume they are bulletproof and totally indestructible. Small children have incredible imaginations and absolutely no capacity to envision they could possibly fail at anything. Small children have a natural capacity for Thinking Big. It's the adults, the teachers, and the other assorted crabs in their young lives who are beating down their imaginations and killing their dreams. We systematically reprogram their minds to replace curiosity with mediocrity. We teach them conformity.

Excuse me; this is the United States of America and Americans are born competitors. And we have a history of winning.

Years ago, my son, Zachary, played t-ball. (T-ball is beginners' baseball for five- and six-year-old children, mostly boys. Instead of having a pitcher, the kid stands at the plate and hits a ball off of a tee.) It's hilarious to watch. At that age, children are not yet completely focused and they tend to be somewhat uncoordinated. Truthfully, if one of the kids were to hit the ball directly to the pitcher (the kid who stands where a pitcher would have been), it would probably be an infield home run.

T-ball is one of those events where young kids are supposed to learn skills and teamwork and the importance of winning—at least, that's the way I pictured it. The year Zach played, they threw a big pool party for the team at the end of the season. All of the kids and their parents showed up for hot dogs, Cokes, and party games. It was an opportunity to say goodbye until next season.

Then the coach gathered up the team one last time and conducted a little ceremony where he said something memorable about each of the kids, and then he gave each kid on the team a trophy. He even gave a trophy to the little kid who urinated right in the middle of center field during a Saturday game, right in front of all of the parents and spectators. We're talking about the same little kid who liked to sit in center field during a game and fill his glove up with dirt and throw it up in the air.

Watching the coach give that particular kid a trophy sent me into orbit. You will rarely ever see me as angry as I was on that occasion. My kid was a fairly good t-ball player and he deserved his trophy. But why were we giving a trophy to this kid? I'm sorry. I just don't get it. I never will understand the concept of rewarding losers just because they showed up. What kind of message is that? Did that child learn anything about teamwork or winning? Twenty years later he'll show up in the work force, still goofing off, and still expecting a free trophy.

Did you ever wonder why so many young people are not able to function in today's society? They're not being taught pride in personal achievement and personal accomplishment. They've never been taught to respect winning. Is it any wonder they never develop the entrepreneurial mind-set?

A few years later, I refused to let Zach play soccer in the community soccer league because some of the mothers had gotten together and voted not to keep score during the games. I interpreted that to mean, "We endorse losing."

It's sad. Those kids will go through life aiming at low goals with no appreciation of the exhilaration of being a winner at anything. If you've ever wondered why more and more kids today appear to be low achievers, maybe that's the way we raise them these days.

An immigrant coming to this country has an overwhelming statistical edge over those of us who were born here. I read somewhere that immigrants have a 72 percent greater probability of becoming a millionaire than a native-born American. Could it be the reason they have a statistically greater probability of success is perhaps because many of them have known hardship and suppression? Maybe, they came from a place where they didn't have this abundance of freedom and opportunities. Maybe they're aggressively building their futures and working hard instead of waiting around for something to be given to them. Maybe they don't expect to be rewarded for failure. Maybe, wherever they came from, only the winners got the trophies.

There is one of those sporting equipment supermarkets near my home. They've got this really challenging, extremely difficult rock-climbing wall. Every Saturday, fifty-two weeks a year, there are hundreds of people waiting in line to challenge the wall. Sometimes it may be two hours after you signed up initially before you get a shot at it. Very few people make it even half-way up before they become fatigued. One after another, they fall off of the wall and are lowered down by their safety harnesses. I am proud to say my son, Zachary, has made it to the top of the wall and rung the bell at the top on four different occasions, which, by the way, is every time he ever attempted it. They gave him a tee shirt that says, I Climbed the Wall. That shirt has become a trophy, one of his proudest possessions. I would doubt if even one person out of fifty who sets out to climb the wall ever makes it to the top even once in their lifetime, much less four times. Zach is not particularly athletic but strength alone is not what gets you to the top. My son got to the top of the wall four times because there was no other option in his mind but to make it all the way. He willed his way to the top when others gave up. There were many people who made an attempt to do it, who were physically able, but they weren't committed enough to get there. They could have done it but they gave up. I have taught my son to have Heart.

Eagle Scout

I am fairly certain that most of you are not going to put this book down and run out and join the Scouts. If you have children, however, I strongly advise you to get them involved in scouting.

In my Prosperity Seminars, I try to get people to see the value of raising children to appreciate entrepreneurial values. There are many activities and organizations that will prepare children to develop focus and character. For me it was the Scouts. Ross Perot, Sam Walton, Gerald Ford, and many others—some of the wealthiest and most successful people of our time and some of our greatest leaders—were also Eagle Scouts.

When I was a kid, becoming an Eagle Scout was one of my all-consuming goals. Scouting taught me some of the most valuable, enduring lessons of my life. The values of honor and integrity are at the heart of the scouting philosophy. Scouting is a blueprint for successful living. I still list the fact I am an Eagle Scout very high on my resume as one of my life's proudest accomplishments.

The last gladiator

Most of us have seen the old newsreel clip on the History Channel. Babe Ruth stepped to the plate and pointed to the right field fence. He called his shot. And when the ball sailed over the right field fence the crowd went wild.

Winning is important. If you have children, now is the time to start developing their minds and attitudes. Attitude is everything. It is the essential ingredient to winning.

I'm a competitor. As I often tell my audiences, I am the last gladiator. If you see me in the game, you can believe I came to win. I play everything in life like that. If I don't win, it's okay as long as I know I went for it.

Stop the presses! This is incredible, absolutely ironic. Eerie! I have to believe this is an omen. You might not believe what I am about to write. If I were reading this, I would be skeptical but I swear to you, this is not something I am putting into the book just to make it more colorful. This is really happening.

It is a Sunday afternoon here in Atlanta and the television playing in the background across the room here in my office is tuned to the Superstation. The movie *Rocky II* is playing. Here's where it gets eerie. In the movie Adrian (Rocky's wife) just came out of her coma in the hospital. They just saw their new son for the first time and she asked Rocky to come closer and she looked into his eyes and said, "I want you to win." Just as I was writing this chapter about winning and competition, *Rocky II* comes on the television.

You know, it might sound funny to you, but right now, as I write these words, tears are rolling down my face and I am laughing out loud. I have seen all of the Rocky movies at least a zillion times but they never cease to affect me this way. Right now, I am still watching the movie as Rocky is training, lifting weights, doing one-arm pushups, and running through the streets. The theme music is playing and here I am, sitting at my desk, in front of the word processor, cheering and laughing out loud. This is the same incredible feeling I always feel when it gets to this part of the movie. I love winners. Winning feels good!

Know God

Many rich people do not have a relationship with God. If you're ever going to be prosperous, you've got to believe in something bigger than yourself. That won't make sense to you until you realize that prosperity means more than money and material wealth. This is a key philosophy, a requirement. You must have a relationship with God before you can unlock the vault. It is a basic element in the Equation.

I believe everyone has to have a spiritual base. I choose to be a Methodist. But no matter what your religion is, I believe it's probably all about the same God anyway. I can't imagine God—the Supreme Being, the all-knowing, all-powerful, all-seeing God—would have created all of those different religions. Religion is the creation of men and is the result of men's schemes. It is a shame to think people have created so many different religions in an attempt to separate and control each other. If you are to have freedom of religion, you have to respect others' right to believe in whatever they choose.

Regardless of your religion, whether you are a Christian or of any other faith, you have to believe in something. If you are to ever become totally successful and prosperous, there must be a higher source in your life. In this complex and diverse world, there are thousands of different religions and beliefs. I will never interfere with your right to believe or not believe in whatever you choose, and I demand that you respect my right to believe.

I believe in order to receive true prosperity, you must believe that everything you have and everything you accomplish are gifts from your God. You must accept as truth that God gave you the ability to think and reason. I speak with God every day.

There is no doubt in my mind that God expects us to prosper. If you read the Bible, in The Parable of the Talents, you'll notice the only servant who was punished was the one who buried his talent and did not increase his wealth.

I always become frustrated when I hear the same old tired, sanctimonious crowd of Pharisees trying to tell me there is something unholy, sacrilegious, or un-Christian about becoming a financial success. For the first twenty-five years of His life, Jesus was a carpenter, which was one of the ultimate high-tech professions of the day. If you've ever visited the Holy Land, you may have noticed there is a noticeable scarcity of trees. Jesus, the carpenter, was most likely a highly paid businessman. He probably sold his work and He probably even negotiated deals as He conducted the family business.

This short chapter is the only reference I will make to religion because I believe your beliefs are something personal to you. I am sure you didn't buy this book to receive a sermon about my religion, so I won't give you one.

I don't believe you will ever be truly prosperous without God. I couldn't write this book without saying this. It needed to be said and that's that. Now, let's move on.

Have a lasting and meaningful relationship

If you're just doing this by yourself, for yourself, and only for yourself, it probably won't really mean anything to you when you get there. A stable relationship is a key element in the Equation. This is a piece of puzzle most people overlook.

Sure, I was already in the process of becoming successful before I met my wife, but the real wealth and prosperity came later. You see it is possible to be wealthy without ever becoming prosperous. All of my personal victories and all of my business successes have been influenced by my relationship with my wife, Debbie. Each day I am building a legacy for my son, Zachary. My greatest treasure in this physical plane does not end with the fact that I love them; but it also lies in the fact that I am loved and appreciated by them. The elation and euphoria driving my life is rooted in the fact I have them to share it with.

Certainly there have been many people throughout history who have achieved riches and material wealth without having a family or any kind of a significant relationship. You don't have to be loved to become rich. Scrooge's wealth never made him happy until he shared it with people he cared about. Financial prosperity is just one of the pieces of the puzzle. Prosperity is a total package. It is possible to have wealth without having prosperity. Prosperity requires love.

Work ethic

Time management, discipline, and a good work ethic are basic elements of the Equation. As I mentioned earlier, this book is written for those people who are willing to do what others are not willing to do to get what they say they want. It has been my experience that most people who say they want to be wealthy are not willing to pay the price.

Work ethic is one of the four basic cornerstone pillars of prosperity. We are living in a world where the losers are looking for instant wealth, instant success, and instant happiness with no investment of time or energy on their part. In my experience, they are not willing to work as hard or as long as it takes. Achieving prosperity requires dedication and sacrifice. Most people would rather wish upon a lottery ticket than take their destiny into their own hands.

Prosperity is about a philosophy and a winning mind-set. If you are not success or achievement motivated, don't waste your time dreaming about financial independence. Go home and get some rest! You've got a clock to punch in the morning. Cheer up! The weekend is right around the corner. What the heck, maybe, if you still have the receipt, you might be able to get a refund on this book.

Unless you've read the first part of this book with an objective mind, you'll never be able to grasp the mechanics of prosperity and personal wealth, which I am about to outline in the succeeding parts. Success is more about a philosophy and a mind-set than it is about the mechanical techniques for attaining wealth.

Part Two of
The Prosperity
EQUATION

My Story

This is the rags-to-riches story, from the beginning to the present. Part two of the Prosperity Equation is my personal story of how a kid from the west side of Jacksonville busted out of a bad situation, built three corporations, and made a fortune.

There are many lessons hidden inside of the stories about the traps and pitfalls you will encounter on the road to wealth. From humble beginnings to the heady elation of success, from celebration to the sobering downfall, then climbing back up out of the abyss, my story is filled with the kind of personal adventures only a real entrepreneur could appreciate.

Broke, divorced, and angry

April 28, 1982. I was broke. Divorced. Angry. I was sneaking out of my apartment in the middle of the night, packing my every possession into my old buy-here, pay-here car. I wrapped the mattress and box springs in clear plastic and tied them to the roof.

It was a dark, drizzly night. I was depressed and lonely; my credit was ruined, and my life was in the toilet. With less than four hundred dollars to my name, I was leaving my home in

Jacksonville, Florida, the city where I grew up. I was leaving behind lifelong friends and family, some great memories and some bad memories.

Driving through the night toward Atlanta, a place I had only visited once in my life, I had a lot of time to think. Here I was thirty-five years old, starting over again...again.

Starting over again...again

It was a seven-hour ordeal driving from Jacksonville to Atlanta. Coffee stains were splattered all over the front of my tee shirt. I used to smoke, and even now I can still vividly see myself rooting around in the ashtray, relighting and smoking cigarette butts, carefully picking out the longest, freshest ones first.

I was one miserable human being. Every little event in my life had become a major irritation magnified a thousand times in intensity. Every little setback increased my frustration. It couldn't get any worse than this. This must be the bottom. As I became increasingly angrier about my situation, I held some highly emotional one-on-one discussions with myself.

The power of affirmations

That night, alone and saturated with solitude, I made several decisions that have affected the rest of my life. First of all, I swore I would never find myself in that position again.

The second promise I made to myself that evening had an even greater effect on the rest of my life. I said these words over and over again with feeling and passion, "I will study my profession (sales) as surely as if I were studying for a master's degree in any other profession."

I repeated all of these statements to myself until they became an anthem, a proclamation of determination. "I will be a success." Within five years I was a millionaire.

> "Being poor sucks! I've tried it several times. I gave it a fair shot. I didn't like it! And I swear this will never happen to me again."

I arrived in Atlanta in the heart of the morning rush hour, just as the sun was coming up over the skyline. There were eight lanes of bumper-to-bumper traffic moving in two directions. I had never seen anything like this. The city was alive. I could feel its pulse. It was magic. Something inside told me my dreams were about to come true.

Obsessed with success

Determined to become wealthy, I thought constantly about success and prosperity. I was driven, continuously reprogramming my mind and my attitude. I told myself, over and over again, you are who you think you are...you will tend to become the people you hang around...if you are going to succeed, you must remove the negative people from your life. It wasn't like I had never been a success in the past. At a very young age I had enjoyed a successful career as a radio advertising executive, a record-breaking salesman. In those early years I had been a nationally known radio announcer and promotions director for one of the largest radio stations in the country. All of those experiences have contributed to my later successes.

This time it was going to be different. I was going to build something solid. This time success was going to last.

Sell something

If you're ever going to be rich, if you genuinely, really, truly, honestly want to become rich, you've got to be able to sell something. If you are afraid of sales and marketing or unwilling to tackle these challenges, chances are you will find prosperity elusive, even unobtainable. I know many talented people who never quite made it because they didn't like sales and marketing.

When I arrived in Atlanta back in the spring of 1982, I had no idea where I was going to live or exactly how I was going to survive. All I knew was that I was a professional salesman and I had faith it would all work out.

I met some good friends in Atlanta. They helped me get on my feet.

As a car salesman, I was making big money right out of the chute. I was obsessed with success. I was absolutely determined to become the very best, the absolute very best.

Working long, hard hours, nights and weekends, I studied my profession and paid my dues. Over the next four years, I went from selling cars to becoming one of the top-performing retail automobile dealership managers in the country. Before long, I was able to build an impressive resume, which included a track record as a top manager with several of the largest, most successful automobile dealerships in the country.

At this precise moment I was more focused and driven than I had ever been at any other time in my entire life. I had soon developed a world-class track record for profitability and innovation.

Someday I just might write another book about how I did that. I will give you a hint though: Behind many successful people, there is usually someone else pushing them forward (and helping to spend their money). I dedicate this book to my wonderful wife, Deborah, who has put up with me for nearly twenty years now.

Ziegler Supersystems, Inc.

By spring of 1986, I had earned the reputation as one of the most innovative, profitable, and productive managers in the Atlanta market. My income had climbed high up into the middle six figures, and we were enjoying an extremely comfortable lifestyle.

That was one of the most inventive and creative times in my life. My mind was operating in warp drive, operating at hyperspeed. After all, I had been working on the concept for several years. Now I was ready to make the final commitment, to take the giant step out into space. I was prepared to make the dream into a reality. There was a lot of adrenaline in that decision.

Nearly fifteen years ago, Deborah and I made the decision to start a business, and Ziegler Supersystems Incorporated was born on the kitchen table. It was the beginning of the roller coaster ride that has become the greatest adventure of our lives. We have lived every moment of it. There were times when we experienced heady euphoria as the business soared extremely high and then there were times of despair when we almost crashed and burned. Through it all, this was our baby and it gave us freedom.

The entire Supersystems concept and philosophy had been laid out in writing years before we ever started doing business. There were stacks of legal pads filled with notes and ideas. I had been carefully planning the business long before I actually brought the company into reality. When the decision was made to go for it, I was ready.

From the very beginning, it was all pure concept and innovation. I was going to become a consultant and public speaker. The plan was to build nationally recognized credentials building on the foundation I had established with my retail management track record in Atlanta. At the time, there were no other companies in existence with a similar model.

It was very difficult writing the first textbook. I remember how I struggled to get my thoughts on paper. Mostly they were all new concepts and ideas. A lot of my sales and management approaches were fresh and radical departures from the old standard, traditional ways many of the dealers in the industry were doing business. But when it was finally finished, I had written more than a hundred pages of original material on automobile finance, and I felt good about it. Now, for the first time, I had created something tangible we could sell. We sent the book off to the printer and I hit the streets with little more than a shoeshine and a smile to begin selling our first seminar.

The first seminar

My first Automobile Finance Management Seminar was an overwhelming success! Well, let me back up and restate that last statement. It was sort of successful. I guess it all depends on how you look at it. The good news was we had seventeen attendees at the first seminar. The bad news was only two of them were paying customers. The other fifteen people in that room were complimentary, no-charge seats. Most of the students in our first seminar were personal friends of mine who were attending the seminar at no charge. Of course my wife, Deborah, was there. Fifteen of the people in the first seminar were there simply to give the only two paying students the illusion they were attending a popular event.

Another reason I packed the crowd was because I desperately needed the credibility. Even though the first seminar lost money, we came out of it with a lot of great photographs of me doing a successful seminar before an enthusiastic audience of industry professionals. These photographs, taken by my wife, gave us instant visual validity when I used them later in the advertising pieces I produced for other seminars.

Moving out of the house

Early on, our business skyrocketed. Ziegler Supersystems was immediately profitable. As a matter of fact, the company was growing so fast, I knew it was only a matter of time before we would have to move the business out of the house and find a permanent business location. Our first offices were in the Northlake section of Atlanta. The lease was a three-year commitment with a bail-out option to pay three additional months' rent and walk out after the first year if things didn't go well.

The new Ziegler Supersystems, Inc., offices and training facility consisted of an inner office, an outer office, a small break room, two restrooms, and a classroom for my seminars. The classroom paid the rent because I was saving money by not having to rent hotel meeting rooms for my seminars. We bought used and off-lease furniture on credit cards from a furniture rental company. The training room was outfitted with folding tables, a dry-erase whiteboard, and a standup speaker's podium. There was no turning back now; we were committed and I liked it that way. This little office represented our total commitment to success. There was no other choice; we had to make this thing fly.

Jewels and furs

By the end of 1987, Ziegler Supersystems, Inc., was starting to rock-and-roll. That year, for our anniversary, Deborah and I gave each other gifts that are still among our most cherished possessions. I gave her a full-length Dior mahogany ranch mink coat, with matching gloves, a matching puff beret hat, and a mink purse. She gave me five karats of diamonds set in a seventeen-diamond gold man's ring.

The furs and the jewelry were symbolic. This was a Cinderella story about a guy with a high-school education who grew up on the rough side of a rough town and managed to break out and rise above it all. It was about a guy who got smacked down hard, several times, and kept getting back up. It was about rubbing the magic lamp and getting all of your wishes. Five years after blowing into town with only four hundred dollars to my name, my wife and I were now giving each other twenty-thousand-dollar gifts.

That year I began writing featured articles in one of the national trade publications. Once again, I was manufacturing my own credentials, establishing myself as a nationally recognized expert in the industry. Later, I managed to get a national contract with Ford Motor Company to appear on some of their national training videos. Ziegler Supersystems was on fire.

By 1988 Supersystems was becoming huge. I found myself traveling continually, from coast-to-coast, speaking and consulting. The money was literally rolling in. The good times had arrived.

Movin' on up

By the beginning of 1991, there was no doubt about it: Ziegler Supersystems, Inc., had arrived. Everything we touched was turning to gold. We had thirty high-dollar employees working in upscale offices in a beautiful steel and glass high-rise office building right in the center of the prestigious Dunwoody section of North Atlanta. Deborah had outdone herself decorating. The furniture was perfect. I was so proud of what we had accomplished here.

By this time I was driving my second brand-new Lincoln Town Car, Signature Edition, a far cry from what I drove into town with nine years earlier.

I was wearing a diamond-studded gold Rolex Presidential that was actually a gift from one of our clients. I bought Debbie the ladies' version just like it.

Our son, Zachary, was now walking and talking. He was becoming this neat little person with an incredible personality. Our life was going great. It doesn't get any better than that.

By this time Supersystems had put together a strong sales organization. We had more than a dozen salespeople telemarketing my seminars and consultancies. We were mailing out thousands of flyers and newsletters, and making thousands of phone calls. Our follow-up was incredible.

Constantly in demand, I was booked for speaking engagements with dealer associations, state conventions, and trade functions. No longer just contributing occasional articles, I was now a nationally known columnist writing articles in one of the foremost trade publications in the industry. Every month we ran half-page ads in several of the national trade magazines. Occasionally we even ran full-page ads promoting the seminars and consultancy program.

When it all comes crashing down
around your ears…scramble

On December 5, 1991, Deborah walked into my office and said, "Jim, we are over a half-million dollars upside down with short-term debt. We owe most of it to Diner's Club, American Express, and the IRS, and it's all due immediately."

If there's one thing that every businessperson should be prepared for, it's the possibility that, sooner or later, when the blitz is on and the line breaks down, you might have to forget about the play you were planning and just scramble. This section is about one of those times.

Who would have thought Saddam Hussein would have had the testicular fortitude to invade Kuwait? Watching the Gulf War live on CNN was like living in a slow-motion bad dream. Predictably, the U.S. economy went to hell almost overnight. In those days our consulting business was tied in directly to a percentage of the profits our clients generated. In other words, if our clients weren't making a profit, then neither did we. Unfortunately, 99 percent of our consulting business was with automobile dealerships. During Operation Desert Shield and Operation Desert Storm, automobile sales didn't just slow down, everything virtually ground to a screeching halt. Our company revenues were suddenly nonexistent.

Looking back and second-guessing myself, I now realize I had tried to hang in there too long. In truth, I should have cut my losses and run a lot sooner than I did.

We were bleeding money out of every artery

We went through our cash on hand before I could put a tourniquet on it to stop the bleeding. I was starting to feel like the coyote in the *Roadrunner* cartoons. Whichever way I turned, someone was blowing me up again.

I had the ball, the blitz was on, and my receivers were covered; it was time to scramble.

The first thing I did was terminate all of the employees. I brought all of the consultants home, fired the bookkeeper, and renegotiated with the building management company who generously agreed to allow us to break the lease and move into a smaller space in the same building.

With everything that was happening, the stress was overwhelming. One night I was lying in bed quivering and shaking uncontrollably. My heart was racing in what seemed to be a dead flutter and my pulse was pounding at my temples. It was only an anxiety attack. When it passed, I shot straight up in bed at three in the morning. There was no way I would be able to sleep until I resolved this thing. My mind was spinning out of control. *There's got to be some way out of this!* My wife and I got up out of bed and sat at the kitchen table. By the time the sun came up we had formed our battle strategy. We came up with an action plan to work our way out of this mess.

The plan was to tackle first things first. Our initial phone calls gave us the impression American Express was going to be the most difficult creditor to deal with. We owed them more than sixty thousand dollars, all due immediately. American Express allowed me to pay off the balance in installments with a minimum payment of ten thousand dollars a month, and never put any derogatory credit references in my credit bureau file. Even though we paid off the balance as agreed, they still canceled my corporate card and, to this day, they have never issued me a new account. But at least they allowed me to work my way out of it. I suppose it could have been a lot worse.

The balance on the Diner's Club Card was just a shade more than twenty thousand dollars. Even though the payment was extremely late, they worked with us. We managed to pay off the full balance within 90 days. The people at Diner's Club were wonderful. They understood what was happening to us, and they even allowed me to keep the account after we paid the balance. Not only am I grateful to Diner's Club, but I have been very loyal to them because of the way they worked with me when I was in trouble.

Negotiating with the tax lady

The Internal Revenue Service was the only creditor I was really afraid of. You see, we had taken money out of our employees' checks for their withholding taxes but we hadn't remitted any of those fourth quarter withholdings to the IRS. This could have been considered a criminal act. Of course, I could have copped out and shifted the blame to my bookkeeper. In truth, I honestly did not know how serious the problem was until it was too late. I was not aware of all of the facts. As with everything I do in my life, I chose to accept responsibility, no excuses, and face this thing head-on.

I guess I should point out here our house (actually, it was Deborah's house) already had a second mortgage. We had drawn out all of the equity in the house months ago. Somewhere along the line we had stacked up another hundred thousand in credit card debt. Each one of our credit cards was maxed to the limit.

There was also the matter of a signature loan from Eastside Bank with a twenty-thousand-dollar balance payable on the first of February. There was little hope we would be able to produce financial statements showing enough positive cash flow for the bank to justify rolling it over.

Facing a seemingly insurmountable mountain of negative debt loads, with only five thousand dollars left in the company account, I was certainly in no position to pay the IRS any part of the quarter million I owed them.

When I explained to the woman at the Internal Revenue Service office we had taken withholding taxes from our employees' checks and not remitted them, I was expecting to be handcuffed, dragged down the hallway, and thrown in a dark, moldy dungeon somewhere in the basement of the Federal Building. Needless to say, I was terrified. Not that I had done anything deliberately or maliciously, but all the same, I was responsible.

It wasn't as bad as I had anticipated. She said the IRS probably wouldn't even contact us at least until July or so. She suggested we float the debt until the computers caught up with us. In others words, she was trying to tell us we had time to raise the money. I told her I didn't think we'd be able to have that much, even by July, so I wanted to set up a repayment plan immediately. We had to pay back to the IRS a minimum amount of ten thousand a month with an incredibly high penalty and interest rate. Since I had voluntarily approached them with the problem first, they were actually very pleasant and worked with us on this situation. I had heard all of these horror stories about the IRS, but my experience with them was a positive one. I was honest and straightforward with them; and they gave me a break.

The greatest lesson I learned throughout this ordeal was how much I needed my wife to handle the accounting and bookkeeping. This all happened at a time when our son, Zachary, was just a baby and Debbie was trying to stay at home and become a full-time mom. As I will say many times in the course of my speeches and my writings, "My job is to make the money. I am very good at it. It's counting it I have a big problem with!"

It felt like everything was stacking up against me now. Business looked bleak and, I even considered bankruptcy (for about half a second). The attorneys, the accountants, and all of the experts were recommending bankruptcy. Deborah and I even discussed it, but in our minds, it was never an option. We made up our mind to fight our way out of this thing. Sure bankruptcy would have been the easy way out but we weren't going to do it. We hadn't worked this hard and we hadn't come this far to throw it all away now.

Selling our way out of trouble

On Thursday, January 2, 1992, I sat down at my desk and implemented stage two of the plan. One of my consultants, a middle-aged fellow named Al, had agreed to stay on with me even though he was fully aware I was not going to be able to pay him. Even now, as I write these words, I am smiling when I think about what he did for us back then. Al worked ten hours a day, seven days a week, expecting no paycheck, and of course Deborah was still hanging in there too.

Looking at the business calendar, there was only five thousand dollars in total future business. That was all of the income we had scheduled on the books as far as I could see into the future. We had no pending business, just one measly five-thousand-dollar consulting trip. Things couldn't have looked much worse.

I started making phone calls. This is when I first developed the habit of making a hundred calls a day. I was calling everyone who had ever done business with us. My consultant was handing me the files and the phone numbers. He was writing the results and the follow-up information on a big, dry-erase whiteboard that was hanging on the wall. We called it the War Board.

In less than ten days I had raised more than 160,000 dollars in short-term consulting business and seminar seats. The War Board in my office was filled with new business we would be paid on within the next 120 days. The Gulf War was behind us now and our clients were also anxious to get their businesses back together. Things were looking up and the economy was looking brighter.

> "There's nothing on Earth you can't sell your way out of."

That experience taught me lifelong lessons about the dangers of growing beyond your money. I was living on the corporate edge. There were no reserve funds to weather a big storm. The most enduring lesson I learned throughout the entire ordeal was there's nothing on Earth you can't sell your way out of. That is now the title of one of my signature speeches.

To my credit, and especially because of the efforts of my wife, we were able to pay off all of the debt in only fourteen months. Even through all of that, we've never had any bad credit in our personal or corporate credit files. Our personal and business credit today is absolutely perfect. We have backup credit lines in place right now, which give us the ability to raise millions on short notice.

It was really tough but we did it. In less than two years, we were able to sell our way out of the biggest disaster of our lives, and we were able to keep our credit and reputation perfect. We could have taken the easy way out and walked away from it, but we didn't. I am very proud of that. Many people would have thrown in the towel.

There are many lessons to be learned from this story and the ups and downs we endured as we grew. When things get tough, attack them. You can always find a way to sell your way out of most problems in business. I have seen many people retreat when it gets tough. Never try to account your way down into a profit. There comes a point when cost cutting can kill sales. If you find yourself facing a financial dilemma, you need to formulate a business strategy and aggressively sell your way out of it.

As for Al, he stayed on with me for another two years (on the payroll), and after a while I was even able to hire some of the other consultants back.

Pay your taxes!

As for the IRS, listen carefully to what I am about to say. Pay your taxes! Don't spend a disproportionate amount of time trying to be cute or creative in sheltering your assets and income. Take all of your legitimate earned deductions but don't mess with these people. In my experience, the IRS was fair and they worked with us because we were straight with them. We admitted we had a problem and they offered us a solution. Don't ever give them a reason to come after you.

It took me twenty-five years to become an overnight success

Through the years, I've had more than a thousand different consulting accounts. We've taken trips to big cities and to small towns. I have performed more than three hundred seminars and more than two hundred platform speaking events. I have traveled to destinations in all of the forty-eight continental states as well as Hawaii. One of these days I will make it to Alaska.

I have a map of the United States hanging over my head on the wall behind my desk with several thousand pins in it chronicling my travels. Sometimes I sit at my desk with my hands clasped behind my head and stare at the map in total awe. It is incredible. I had never even flown in an airplane until I was thirty years old and now here I am looking at several thousand pins on a map. It's hard to believe I've actually been to all of these places. Somewhere back there in the late eighties I made a decision I would only fly first-class and I would only stay in upscale hotels. Today all of my travels are 100 percent first class, 100 percent client reimbursed.

In 1996, long after Supersystems had become an established success story with a national track record, we started the second company, Ziegler Dynamics, Inc.

Dynamics is a corporation dedicated to the public speaking business and consulting in industries other than the automobile industry. Ziegler Dynamics works with a variety of businesses. We specialize in cosponsored events with chamber of commerce clients. My specialty is how to start and grow a small business. Once again, we have employed the same strategies and concepts that originally made Supersystems successful. As soon as Dynamics was up and running, I immediately set out on a campaign to create credentials and publicity campaigns for James A. Ziegler, professional speaker. Through radio appearances, national television interviews, writing articles in national magazines, and being quoted in national newspapers, I began to establish myself as a national expert in business and marketing. High visibility in and of itself is a valuable credential with collateral value.

From day one we created first-class videos and promotional materials. As with Ziegler Supersystems, Ziegler Dynamics' collateral materials have always been centered on a first-class presentation. When you are creating your company image, this is not the time to cut corners or get cheap.

Each of my companies has its own dedicated multimedia Web site. Currently I have three more registered Web sites under construction. My advice to any entrepreneur who is looking to start a new business is…embrace technology.

The Prosperity Seminars

The Prosperity Seminars, which are starting to play a major role in our business, just sort of happened. I really wasn't looking for another profit center when this idea just showed up knocking at the door demanding for me to take a look at it.

After more than twenty-five years as a successful, high-dollar, professional speaker, late one night I was rooting around on the Internet and stumbled across the Web site for the National Speakers Association. I never even knew there was such an association. Joining NSA has become one of the most rewarding experiences of my entire career. Imagine what is was like when I attended my first national convention and got to know the gods of my profession. Zig Ziglar, Harvey McKay, Tony Allesandra, Jim Cathcart, Patricia Fripp, Dan Kennedy, Les Brown, Tom Antion, Brain Tracy, and thousands of others. Being a member of NSA was like having a backstage pass to a rock concert and getting to meet all of your favorite stars firsthand. The knowledge I've gained and the lifelong friendships that have grown out of the NSA experience have boosted me to yet another level. Here I was networking with my peers and finding new mentors.

When I joined NSA, I quickly learned there is a prestigious award called the Certified Speaking Professional designation. This is the highest earned award that can be bestowed upon a member of the organization. The CSP is a difficult goal and requires professional achievements and a higher level of performance. Less than 5 percent of the organization's membership ever reaches this level. It is every professional speaker's goal. This year I have finally met all of the requirements and qualified for this honor. It is one of my proudest accomplishments.

As a byproduct of my successes, I began to meet a lot of people who were still piecing together their personal puzzle. Barely a week passes that there is not someone sitting in my office asking for advice about his or her business. I've had groups of people caravan several hundred miles just to meet with me and tour my offices to see how we do business. I love coaching others to be successful.

Two years ago I conducted a test seminar on marketing and sales just to see if there was any market for these seminars. Hundreds of people showed up with very little up-front advertising. We filled three hundred seats in a downtown amphitheater with opportunity seekers and small business people.

The test seminar proved two things. The first thing we learned was that the market for these Prosperity Seminars is enormous. The opportunities were potentially unlimited. The second thing I realized was I was very good at it. Shortly thereafter I began writing this book.

The dream house

Throughout all of the ups and downs, bumps and grinds, and hiccups we experienced in the first seven years in business, we were still living in the little wooden frame house Deborah's father had built for her before we met. It was a beautiful little home in a nice residential neighborhood.

When Zachary was born, being good parents was our primary mission. We were very content, for the time being, to stay where we were.

Even though we weren't actually in the market, we loved to spend Sundays driving through some of the new upscale communities that were springing up all over Atlanta. It was exciting to walk through all of these big new houses in these fabulous country club environments. Most of them were still under various stages of construction. It was our dream that one day we would live in a big wonderful home like one of these.

My wife has excellent taste. She could be a consultant for *Southern Living* magazine if she wanted—she's really that good. Debbie knows what she likes and what she doesn't like. We talked about exactly what kind of a house we would want. Just looking at everything out there gave us a lot of great ideas for floor plans and decorating schemes. We liked the way the kitchen was set up in this one and we loved the vaulted ceiling in the master bedroom in this one and the great room with the fireplace in this one. You get the picture. We were dream shopping.

Then one day, here we were driving through a brand-new community just outside of Atlanta. The homes were huge, built on large, beautifully landscaped lots. I made a right turn just past the clubhouse on a street where they were just starting to frame about five new homes. I swear, I think the house just reached out and backslapped both of us across the face. It was insistent, demanding we stop and take a look at it.

This particular house was already fully framed out on a big, beautiful lot, more than a full acre. As we walked from room to room, I could see Debbie becoming visibly more and more excited. It was more than 4,800 square feet with a spacious two-story great room, with vaulted ceilings and chandeliers. I could fill these pages describing all of the wonderful, modern, and beautiful things about this house. It was exactly everything we had always said we were looking for. Too bad we weren't ready to buy one at this time. Unfortunately, we weren't financially ready to make this commitment. We were just looking.

Just out of curiosity, on the way out of the neighborhood, we stopped and met with the developer who told us all about the builder and the community. I really hated it but there was no way. Not at this time. We just weren't ready to commit to a house like this. Were we? It would take a substantial down payment to float a loan that big, fifty or sixty thousand in cash just for the down payment, and then another sixty or seventy thousand to furnish it. Even though we had built up substantial equity in Debbie's house, we just didn't have that kind of money lying around in liquid cash. Did we? Debbie smiled at me. We did have exactly that much money. As an entrepreneur I have a confession to make. I know how to make a lot of money, an awful lot of money. I've always had the ability to generate huge volumes of cash. My biggest problem is I have no desire, and very little ability, to count it or manage it. When we were dating, Debbie was appalled to find out I sort of kept my checking account balance in my head. That's one of the best reasons I can think of to marry a woman who has a background in accounting.

Where in the heck did she get that much money? Come to find out, Debbie had been squirreling away all of the money from her paychecks from Supersystems for the last couple of years. She had saved more than enough money to get into the new house before we sold the old one.

In 1994, Deborah and I moved into our dream home, a European stucco with more than 4,800 square feet of living space and a three-car garage in a luxury swim-and-tennis community.

Extravagance

Last year we finally finished our basement, with six more rooms and a full bathroom downstairs, adding an extra 3,500 square feet to our home.

There are more than fifteen televisions with VCRs in the house, including two big screens with DVD. We have a fully equipped modern workout room in the new basement area, complete with weights, treadmill, body bag, and a variety of other machines. My personal office downstairs is a rich, burgundy color with vaulted ceiling and upscale furnishings. The office has state-of-the-art computers and office equipment. The family room downstairs features a home theater with built-in quadraphonic sound. There's a new bedroom downstairs, as well as a game room where we are getting ready to put the new pool table. The wet bar in the party room is fully functional with refrigerator, sink, and dishwasher. Everything is furnished extravagantly, in the best of taste.

All of the jewelry, the big house, the cars, the travel, the designer clothes, and the lifestyle we enjoy today are a celebration and a testament to the hard work and teamwork that made it all happen.

Many times I have been accused of being flashy and extravagant. You know what? Really, truly, honestly, I don't care what people think about that. My attitude is: I know how hard I worked to have what I have. I know the risks my wife and I took while other people were choosing to play it safe. My wife and I have invested a lot of sweat and blood and heartache to get to this point. If anyone thinks I am trying to make some kind of a statement. Guess what? They're probably right!

Debt

We stay very nearly debt-free. With the exception of the house payment and car lease payments, we pay off all of our credit accounts, in full, every month. We put airline tickets, hotel tabs, and seminar events on personal cards and then get reimbursed through the corporations. Deborah pays off all of our credit cards, every month, in full.

A word of advice to every startup entrepreneur: Run your business purchases through your credit cards and then pay the balances every month in full. Of course, this only works if you have the discipline to follow the script. This strategy has two great benefits. First, you can float your expenses monthly, interest-free if you pay in full, and have them recorded and itemized. Second, you get to use the buying power of your corporation to get points on the credit cards toward their awards programs.

Five years ago we moved our business back into a larger facility. Since we had that financial hiccup back in 1992, we were understandably cautious about making permanent lease commitments. We moved the companies into a 5,000-square-foot office suite with a large classroom that will seat fifty seminar attendees. When you walk through my offices, everything is first class. Even better, everything is paid for. We own all of the office equipment, furniture, televisions, telephone systems, copiers, computers, and so forth. There is zero contingent liability here. Business is booked as far into the future as I want it to be.

Recently we purchased a new, state-of-the-art (for now anyway) NT Network Computer System with a station on every employee's desk. These computers are so radical they can stand on their back wheels and smoke the tires. This was a major expenditure. We were able to pay cash.

The staff is still small. There are two executive secretaries, one outside consultant, a director of sales and technology, a publicity specialist, and myself. Of course, my wife Deborah still handles the bookkeeping and accountant liaison. We do an extremely high-dollar business with a very small staff.

A nationally known professional speaker

My personal time as a consultant bills for upwards of five thousand dollars per day plus first-class airfare and luxury-class hotel reimbursement as well as in-town transportation paid for by the client.

As a professional speaker, I perform more than twenty-five platform events a year—keynotes and private seminars. At five- to ten-thousand dollars per event, I am booked 250 days a year, speaking and consulting. I am in constant demand as a convention speaker, which creates more consulting business than I can physically get to.

All of these appearances, speaking engagements, and articles and national columns in the magazines were the end result of a calculated business strategy. My business plan is paying off handsomely.

Making money became my top priority

When I blew into Atlanta with the mattresses tied to the roof of that old, beat-up car, I made several life-changing decisions. At age thirty-five, I realized that might be my last chance to get this show on the road. I began to obsess about success. I read every book, listened to every tape, and attended every seminar. I became consumed by the desire to succeed. I ate it, slept it, and drank it. If you are to ever arrive at the level of success I am describing in this book, you must devour success. I think the word I am searching for is *passion.*

To this day, I read at least twenty magazines every week. I read every issue of *Businessweek, Time, Success, Entrepreneur, Fortune, Money,* and *The Wall Street Journal.* Now that these publications are online, there is no excuse for anyone not to be informed and up-to-date.

Today I travel more than 250 days a year, speaking and consulting. If I'm flying on a plane, it is not uncommon for me to read every magazine on the rack. I watch CNBC every morning before I start my workday and often catch programs on CNNfn and Bloomberg.

It's nearly fifty miles from my home to the airport. Sometimes I have to make the trip several times a week. Whenever I am driving alone there is going to be a tape playing in the dash. Through the years I've spent a fortune buying tapes, investing in developing my mind. As a professional speaker and consultant to businesses, the things I know have become the tools in my toolbox. I am paid to be an expert.

When I talk about getting the negative people out of your life, sometimes that is the most difficult part of the Prosperity Equation. It is the one subject I am not going to spend a lot of time discussing in this book because it's very personal to you.

This can be one of those extremely emotional, private one-on-one discussions with yourself that many people are not willing to face. Take a moment and think about it. You're on your own with this one.

Part Three of
The Prosperity
EQUATION

Getting Ready to Get Ready

There are some unique entrepreneurial thought processes I am going to attempt to relate to you as we transition into Part Three of the Prosperity Equation. These are my concepts of how those entrepreneurial realities apply to our businesses. As a business owner, you have definitely stepped over the line into another dimension of perception. Maybe this really is the Twilight Zone. Regardless, you must be prepared to change the way you look at everything when you are in business for yourself. We have passed beyond the philosophies and we are into the actualities of what you must do to get there. The combination to the vault is in the words ahead.

Seek models and mentors

Every book I read, every tape I listened to, said the same thing: If you really want to be successful at anything, seek out the very best people in that field and model yourself after them. To become a super salesman, I had to find super salespeople and study their habits. To become a profitable businessman, I had to study the habits of successful business people who already had solid documented track records for making money.

The concept of leveraging other people's experience entails asking someone to help you who has been there and done that already. A mentor is someone with a proven track record who is willing to coach and advise you.

Think and Grow Rich—*my personal road map*

In my business philosophies, I have many bibles. But *Think and Grow Rich* by Napoleon Hill has become my dominant guiding business philosophy. Saturating my mind with success, even today I often find myself listening to *Think and Grow Rich* on cassette tapes when I am alone in the car.

Even though that book was written more than sixty-five years ago, it is the foundation upon which I built my companies. Today it is still selling in paperback and I give dozens of copies to my friends, employees, and clients. I believe it is one of the most sincere and personal gifts I could give them.

This book is not optional. You must buy it and read it, over and over again, as you prepare your mind to become wealthy and prosperous.

> "Anything a man can conceive, and believe, you can achieve."
>
> —*Napoleon Hill,* Think and Grow Rich

"Anything a [person] can conceive and believe, you can achieve." I have spent many hours thinking about exactly what those words mean and how I can apply them to my life. I have met hundreds of other successful businessmen and businesswomen who have built their companies, and ultimately their fortunes, with the concepts they learned from that book.

More recently there is another book titled *Think and Grow Rich: A Black Choice* by Dr. Dennis Kimbro, an African-American. This book bills itself as "A Guide to Success for Black Americans." Kimbro actually expanded and finished a book that was originally begun by Napoleon Hill, himself, to give Black Americans a personalized blueprint to pursue their dreams and to become prosperous. I have read this book several times and find it inspirational and meaningful to me, even though I am not African-American. It is excellent.

Envision having wealth and believe it

Think and Grow Rich introduced me to conceptual thinking. Imagination is the most valuable personal asset a person can possess. I am talking about the ability to clearly visualize your goals, to be able to visualize having exactly what you want and then to believe you'll actually have it. There is no doubt in my mind that you can think and dream and believe your way into a fortune. I am a firm believer that every self-made wealthy person on Earth began with a believable vision. Creativity is a visual thing.

Years before I actually arrived at the point where I am today, I could clearly see myself living this lifestyle. The journey was always moving toward an inevitable goal. There was never any doubt in my mind this would happen to me. That is what I was talking about when I said most of the Prosperity Equation starts in your head.

> "There is no doubt in my mind that a person can think and dream and believe their way into a fortune."

Quantify your wants

Most people have no idea exactly what it is they really want out of life. One of the exercises we often ask students to do in my seminars is to write out everything that they want, exactly what they want. How can you ever expect to have these things unless you have clearly visualized exactly what it is that you want?

Do you want a house? What kind of house?

You say you want a new car, describe exactly what kind of car.

You say you're looking for financial security. Exactly how much money are we talking about here anyway?

A boat? What kind of boat?

Your own business? Exactly what kind of business?

You want good health? What do you mean by that?

You say you're looking for a meaningful relationship. Exactly what would that mean to you?

Visualize your goals

Someone once told me, "If you don't know where you're heading, then any road will take you there."

Every once in a while you trip over something that, once again, changes everything. When I first read the book *The 7 Habits of Highly Effective People* by Stephen Covey, it was no surprise to me that I had accidentally stumbled onto some of the concepts Covey had written about in the book. I was already living them in my daily life. *7 Habits* was another one of those books that just made me just sit there and say, "Wow!" It was filled with missing pieces to the puzzle I was working on. With Covey's words, "Begin with the end in mind," I could see he was creating expanded concepts built on the foundations other great writers and motivators had already laid down. As I sat there reading Covey's book for the third and fourth time, the words of Napoleon Hill kept echoing and reverberating through my mind, "Anything a [person] can conceive and believe, you can achieve."

 The common threads that run through the teachings of Dale Carnegie, Napoleon Hill, and Stephen Covey: "Visualize having exactly what you want and then believe that you'll have it."

Have you ever seen one of those bumper stickers that read "Visualize world peace"? Well, I visualize success. I can clearly see the future result of what I do today. I know exactly what I will have and where I will be. It is extremely real to me. There is no doubt. I truly believe you are what you think about.

If life hands you a disappointment, make an adjustment and move on. This is more than simply being bright and cheery and optimistic. I am a realist. Of course there are going to be setbacks in life. Your plans are not always going to materialize exactly the way you've planned them. So what? Even during the very worst times I can recall, over the course of my entire life, quitting was never one of my options. Failure is always a possibility. Quitting is not.

I want more

When you were a kid, did you read any comic books about Walt Disney's Scrooge McDuck? Even as I am sitting here writing this, I am chuckling to myself as the visual flickers in my memory. Scrooge McDuck was Donald Duck's uncle. As you might remember, the Beagle Boys were always plotting to steal Scrooge's money. The name "Uncle Scrooge" conjures up images of Ebenezer Scrooge to intensify the stereotype that he was frugal and miserly.

In every issue there was at least one frame where Scrooge was sitting in one of his vaults on top of this tremendous pile of money. There were always vast oceans of coins and bills and gold and silver. Scrooge would be sitting on top of the peak of this mountain of money, just laughing hysterically and throwing his money up into the air, letting it rain down all around him. Sometimes he would be buried in it up to his neck. He could never get enough of it. I love that picture. I could see myself there.

Maybe we'll never attain the ridiculous cartoon wealth of a Scrooge McDuck, but there's one thing you can chisel in granite: I will never be content with the way it is. I want more!

"Goal-setting is clarifying and crystallizing your dream until you can see it in every small detail. People without a defined and measurable goal only have a pipe dream. If your goal is all smoke and mirrors, then you are living in delusion, a negative illusion. You don't really have a goal until you can clearly see your dream."

Focus on your goal

Ziegler's first rule of profit centers is to focus on your goal. In other words, do what you do best and don't take on diverse unrelated projects. All of your profit centers must be interrelated and manageable. Don't run in too many directions all at once.

One of the most powerful business philosophies I learned from reading Napoleon Hill was that wealthy, successful people have the ability to recognize an opportunity when they are looking at it. Most wealthy, successful people can also recognize potential projects that are not opportunities and avoid them. Reading and listening to Napoleon Hill taught me to focus my efforts. In business, a large diversity of unrelated projects becomes unmanageable and will cause you to crash and burn.

Don't try to hang onto something while you're building something else. If you're not prepared to start your business, don't even think about it. You are never going to become wealthy or successful if you are afraid to jump into it without a safety net. Being successful doesn't mean planning to fail and it doesn't mean moving too slowly or too cautiously. If the ride scares you, then don't get on it in the first place. It's like being on a roller coaster. Once you're buckled in and the darn thing starts moving, it's too late to change your mind. It doesn't matter that you're scared. You're committed. The time when you could have chickened out has passed and now there's no turning back. Your only option is to brace yourself and get ready for the ride! You want to be wealthy and successful? You'll never make it unless you develop a risk-taker mentality.

As you begin to become more successful, you are going to be tempted to start many new projects, most of which are unrelated to your core business. You will never be successful if you constantly chase after every new rainbow before you have collected the pot of gold at the end of the last one. In business, once you've earned a reputation as a proven success, they'll start coming out of the woodwork. You will be assailed by many distractions disguised as golden opportunities. Stay focused!

Rarely does a week pass that I don't find myself approached by someone from another company who wants to partner up with me on some fantastic new business venture. Of course, they are asking me to dedicate a lot of my personal energy on a project that doesn't fit into the narrow focus of my business plan. Their proposal might actually be a great idea that would probably make a lot of money, that is, if I chose to pursue it. Usually, I find a graceful way to tell them I am not interested.

Although I rarely enter into contracts and side agreements with other companies or individuals, I never miss an opportunity to make new friends who can help my business. I always end up finding a way to leverage their business contacts as part of my ever-growing circle of influence in my personal and business network.

Of course, even as I sit here writing these words, I know for a fact you won't listen to this advice. Even though I've told you so, you will be doomed to make the mistake of taking your eye off the ball. No matter how many times or how many different ways I say it, this is one of those lessons you'll have to learn the hard way.

I have filing cabinets filled with dead projects I should never have started. Every one of these mind deals looked really good at the time. I am guilty of wasting an incredibly stupid amount of valuable time and money pursuing silly projects and side ventures. The lessons learned have finally sunk in.

Sometimes my employees will come into my office with some great idea about some incredible new profit center we need to get into. They sit there bubbling over with enthusiasm as they present some new, wave of the future concept they are convinced is going to make me a fortune. I always listen. Never kill your associate's creativity or do anything to discourage it. You never know what pearls they might throw at your feet when you least expect it. One of the philosophies I have come to embrace is to keep my mind open and always consider new ideas. Even so, I have also learned to carefully weigh my options before I make even the slightest change in the original game plan.

Who do you know that can help me?

Networking is powerful. Success in life can be measured by the strength of a person's relationships with other people. We are all living in a social world. Your success is directly proportional to the number of people you influence. In other words, the most successful people are those people who have the greatest influence over the largest number of other influential people. I believe your level of success in life and business is directly proportional to your ability to network with other people. In business, as in life, I believe you must be able to leverage your relationships.

> "The most successful people are those people who influence the most other people."

I realized early on that my personality was my strongest personal asset. There are many moments in people's lives they identify as a "turning point," something that had a profound and lasting effect on the direction of their life from that point forward. One of those turning points in my life was the book *How to Win Friends and Influence People* by Dale Carnegie. Sometimes the old wisdom is still the best wisdom. Many of the philosophies influencing the direction my life is taking today originated in the pages of that book.

Even though it was originally published in 1937, *How to Win Friends and Influence People* is a timeless collection of wisdom and usable knowledge.

The first time I read it, it occurred to me that Dale Carnegie was the first person to actually quantify the value of human relationships. Certainly, he was the father of the scientific sales approaches we use today. Human relationships are a science that can be studied, measured, quantified, and improved. Carnegie's techniques for winning people over to your side are the basic building blocks every sales trainer uses today.

In later years when I first took the Dales Carnegie sales course, once again those same lightbulbs light up my mind. Professional sales is a precise and measurable science based on relationships. I highly recommend Dale Carnegie sales training to every beginner in sales and business.

In *The 7 Habits of Highly Effective People*, Stephen Covey introduces the conceptual idea of a person's "circle of influence." Your personal circle of influence is one of the most dynamic forces in your life and in your business.

Climbing the ladder toward prosperity, I was first a highly successful salesman and later became a record-setting sales manger. It was always my ability to prospect for new business and to network with influential people that awarded me my greatest victories. My successes in life and business are directly proportional to my ability to generate new business through referral and personal introduction.

In the business of sales and marketing, it is important to get to the decision makers. I am always looking for a direct link to the top person, the one person who can overrule everyone else about whether or not they will buy the goods or services I am selling. My sales strategy is to start at the top level. Most salespeople start out calling on people at the lowest levels of authority in an organization and then they try to work their way up to an audience with the decision maker. The trouble with this approach is that you have to present your proposal to each level. What I am looking for are those people who can help me with a direct introduction to the decision maker as opposed to a cold call starting out with someone at a lower level in the organization.

In most business environments, the only way to get new business is to take that business away from someone who already has the account. In other words, you must be willing and able to defeat an established relationship between your desired client and a competitor who already has the business you want. This is a delicate situation and you could easily blow it if you are not set up with the right Power Posture going in.

Your Power Posture begins with the total impression your customer has of you and the value they place on you as someone they would want to do business with. It's a respect thing. For more than twenty-five years I have been trying to find the right words to describe this concept. I do know it's got a lot to do with your professionalism and your perceived expertise. Although I have never been able to adequately describe exactly what it is, you need it, and you have to have it to be successful. Let's just suffice it to say, if you have it, you already know it.

Taking business away from an entrenched competitor who already has the account is difficult. You've got to find a way to bypass all of the lower levels of bureaucracy in the company and get your presentation in front of the decision maker, at the very top level. Later on, when you are introduced to the lower-level buyer by the big shot who is in charge, you are coming in as an invited guest. You are a friend of a friend. The atmosphere is warm and your presentation is welcome when someone's superior in his or her own company refers you.

How many salespeople and small business owners have we all known throughout our lives who spent all of their time chasing all of those elusive mind deals? Constantly babbling about incredible sales and deals that were never actually going to happen in the real world? We've all met those small-time operators who are right on the verge of putting together this tremendous sale that is going to be "the mother of all deals."

Gather People

I've been studying and teaching relationship-based marketing for more than twenty-five years. I was teaching these concepts long before every other speaker and paperback writer in the universe recently discovered them. In every one of my lectures and consulting projects I am teaching an original concept principle I call Gather People.

When you are first setting up your personal network, it is important for you to take the time to define specifically who you would like to meet through introduction. Somebody told me one of those ridiculous "folklore factoids" recently. Every human being on the planet is connected, within six generations, to every other human being on the planet. In other words, everyone on Earth knows somebody who knows somebody who knows somebody who knows somebody who knows somebody connecting you within six people to virtually anyone and everyone else on Earth. *Six Degrees of Kevin Bacon* by Fass, Ginelli, and Turtle was based on this assumption. This humorous book chose the actor Kevin Bacon to demonstrate the theory that you can trace everyone on Earth to everyone else through six human links. A few years back the Kevin Bacon Game was an epidemic fad on college campuses.

Say if you really wanted to meet Tom Cruise, theoretically you already know someone who knows someone who knows someone who knows someone who knows someone who knows Tom Cruise. The point is, whether there is any truth behind this silly example or not, you can magnify your circle of influence by finding people who know people who know people you would like to know. Every time I add someone to my personal sphere of influence I am building a bridge to all of the people they know.

Develop allies inside of the company

Once you have met anyone in your industry that might be of help to you in the future, never lose track of him or her. Nobody is too small to be part of your personal network or your company's business network. I'm talking about everyone, at all levels, secretaries, salespeople, assistants, aides, janitors, mechanics, and anyone else who might even remotely come into contact with a decision maker. In my companies, we keep in our database a lot of people you might consider insignificant. It doesn't really matter who they are or what they do. Don't exclude anyone from your list. I try to meet and get to know as many people as is humanly possible in virtually every walk of life. Exclude no one.

Experience has proven many times that my company will ultimately win the business if we are able to build allies within the organization. When I am trying to sell our services to another business, it helps to have friends at every level. You never know when the boss is going to casually mention you or your company in front of a secretary or an employee who is going to say something really positive about your business and swing the deal your way.

Once my company has secured the business, we always try to get the home address and phone number of every person with whom we interacted. Then, if they move onto another employer, we still have the ability to get in touch with them. I can't tell you how many people were so grateful we kept in touch with them after they left their previous employer that they recommended my company to their new employer when they finally landed.

You don't know what you don't know

Bill is a big, friendly guy. We first met him in our adult Sunday school class. Ordinarily, most people, including me, wouldn't associate Bill with a direct link to the top decision makers. He's a blue-collar supervisor with Delta Airlines. Nevertheless, Bill is my friend and Bill knows what I do for a living.

I am a platinum medallion frequent flyer with Delta, a multimillion-mile customer. I always fly full-fare, first class. In other words, my company has done a lot of business with these folks. Even so, I have always found it difficult to break through all of the levels and filters that isolate the officers of the company from their customers.

Debbie and Zach and I were headed to our favorite resort hotel on Grand Cayman Island. It was early Friday morning and we were waiting in the Delta Crown Room before the flight. I quickly recognized Leo Mullin, the CEO of Delta Airlines, sitting by the window of the Crown Room surrounded by a crowd of people. He was doing a photo shoot for the *Delta* magazine.

For personal and business reasons, Leo Mullin was one of those people I really wanted to meet. I didn't feel it would be appropriate to walk up and try to start a conversation. The man was working.

Later on when they took a break to reset the backdrops, you can imagine how surprised I was to see Leo Mullin walking and talking, side-by-side, with my friend Bill. We had stopped and said hello to Bill earlier when we passed him on the way in but it never occurred to me that he was with Leo Mullin. A few moments later, Mr. Mullin walked over to my family and me and introduced himself. We talked one-on-one for maybe twenty minutes. I had an opportunity to sincerely compliment him on the great job I felt he was doing with the airline. A few minutes later, he excused himself and went back to his photo shoot.

After Mr. Mullin went back to the photo shoot, Bill walked over to us wearing his trademark smile. I had told him months ago over coffee that I would really like to meet Leo Mullin. Of course, it never dawned on me at the time that Bill had access to him. As it turned out, Bill was escorting Mr. Mullin around the airport that day. He told us that Mr. Mullin had requested one of my business cards. I gave Bill one of my cards and a one-sheet flyer about my company to give to Mr. Mullin.

Since then I have had a direct link to Leo Mullin. He knows me and I know him. Although I've never had any desire to attempt to contact Mr. Mullin or to leverage the relationship, I do write him a complimentary note every now and then when some Delta employees give extraordinary service.

Losers are a liability

In networking, the people you know and who know you say a lot about who you are, or at least who you appear to be. One of the most difficult things in life is having the strength to get the negative people out of your life. I am talking about the quality of people you choose to allow to become a part of your personal network. Intuition is a powerful thing. If someone appears to be a loser, in all probability, they probably are.

As I mentioned previously, I am a nationally recognized figure in the retail automobile industry. Unfortunately, the car business has given itself more than its fair share of black eyes and bad public relations. In every speech or seminar I have ever performed to managers and salespeople in the car business, I have always said, "You don't need to lie or cheat or sneak or deceive to sell automobiles. If I even suspected that you were dishonest, I would persecute you and run you out of our industry. We don't need criminals in the car business." Every time I say those words in a seminar you can see mouths drop wide open all over the room.

How many people are actually willing to state what you stand for? If you allow losers in your life, it will reflect on you and it will bring you down in the eyes of those people you most want to meet. The quality of the people in your personal network is an asset. Losers are a liability.

> "If you help other people to get what they want, you will receive more than you'll ever need."
>
> —*Zig Ziglar, circa 1970*

Of course Zig originally got this concept from the Old Testament, Eccles. 11:1, which says: "Send out your bread upon the waters for after many days you will get it back."

In the New Testament, Acts 20:35 says: "It is more blessed to give than to receive."

Since Zig got it from the Bible, I don't mind using it here. I consider Zig Ziglar to be one of the greatest speakers and motivators of all time. Reading Zig Ziglar's books and listening to his tapes taught me this basic cornerstone philosophy that has helped me to increase the quality of my life in almost every way. It is a simple basic concept rooted in goodness and kindness: "You will always get what you want by helping other people to get what they want."

There is a big difference in setting up a powerful and productive personal network as opposed to simply using other people to get what you want. You develop personal relationships by doing nice things for other people without a specific reward in mind. Without thinking about a specific reward or personal agenda, try to do good things for others whenever possible. Zig Ziglar is right. Make it a point to help others; it all comes back to you.

One of the habits I believe has greatly elevated my success is when I end every conversation with these words: "Is there anything I can do to help you?" It is important for you to focus on their agenda. How can you help them achieve whatever it is they want?

I have landed hundreds of profitable business opportunities as a result of a conversation I had with someone I met on an airplane. Through the years I have done a lot of business with contacts who were referred to me through personal contacts in my immediate circle of influence.

Building a personal network is a lot easier than keeping it. As an example, how many of those people who were your closest friends and acquaintances in high school are you still in touch with today? How many of them have a clear picture of what you are doing today? Do you know what they're doing today? Do you know if they know anyone you would like to know?

Most people are guilty of wasting all of the personal relationships they've developed over the course of their lives. People you should have gathered and kept in your circle of influence throughout your life gradually slipped away from you and the value of the relationships were eventually lost.

A few years back I hired my young brother-in-law to manage my business. Fresh out of business school, the ink was still wet on his diploma. One day he walked into my office and proudly announced that he had deleted several thousand dead contacts from our database. In other words, he had erased several thousand names of past clients because they had not done business with us over the last few years. Of course, on the surface, his rationale made a lot of sense. We were going to save thousands by no longer sending flyers and newsletters to people who were no longer doing business with us.

Fortunately, I had backed up the entire database and those names were not lost forever. We restored the entire database immediately. You see he didn't know about the relationships I had cultivated with those people through the years. It had taken me nearly fifteen years to put that database together and even though some of those people were no longer doing business with us, they were still referring many new clients. These people still looked forward to reading our literature and flyers. The stuff they were getting from us every month was keeping us in the forefront of their minds. These people were still talking about our company at the meetings and the conventions they attended. These relationships were paying off in many ways he was not aware of.

Get their first name and use it

One of the common characteristics of most wealthy and successful people is their ability to remember people's names and to use people's names when speaking to them. I dedicated many hours developing my ability to remember people's names. At the beginning of my seminars, I ask the people in the audience to cover up their name badges and then I go around the room telling each of them their names. On three occasions I have successfully remembered the names of more than 150 attendees only a half hour or so after I first met them. This requires a lot of focus and concentration.

In my travels, I always learn people's names and use their name when I speak to them. This is another one of those Power-

Posturing techniques. I'm talking about everyone whether or not it's a waiter in a restaurant or a vice president at General Motors. One of the most powerful things I learned years ago in the Dale Carnegie sales course was this simple sentence: "Get their name and use it."

I have expanded the Carnegie concept and created an original James A. Ziegler concept, which is, "Get their first name and use it." In your business and personal relationships, it is essential to break down the barriers between you and other people. One of the greatest barriers in most relationships is getting beyond the other person's title. It is imperative for you to get on a first-name basis with everyone as soon as possible (and only when it is possible). I seldom use the words such as ma'am or mister when I am dealing with other people. I also try avoiding titles like reverend or doctor in my conversations (unless the person is acting in the capacity of a minister or a doctor at that exact moment). My goal is to develop a peer-level relationship with others.

One of the reasons I have arrived at some level of success and affluence is because I have the ability to make other people think I am one of them. You don't gain people's affection or respect by groveling and cowering. I know thousands of top executives on a first-name basis because the relationship started out that way from the first moment.

Deal with the decision makers

Even though I have mentioned it several times already, there's another point I'd like to hammer home. I have always dealt with the owner, the president of the company, the CEO, or the dealer. One of my key philosophies is to establish myself as their peer, someone who is an expert on their level. So many business people approach a client with a weak, wimpy Power Posture. It is important to strategically position the image of your company in your clients' minds. You don't want to be perceived as just another vendor groveling for their business.

As a matter of fact, in my company, I will turn down business if I feel it isn't the right chemistry. One of the funniest jokes I tell prospective clients is that I have fired many more clients than have ever fired us. Never let them smell desperation. Never give a client the impression you absolutely need their business.

As a result of the relationships I have developed over the years, I can pick up a telephone and get more top executives on the phone than just about anyone in my industry. We know each other on a first-name basis. They'll take my call even though their secretaries will screen almost every other caller. I rarely start the deal with subordinate managers or employees. My plan of attack is to always start out dealing with the very top person from the very beginning of the relationship. I will usually continue to do business at that level.

Every event in your life is a photo opportunity

Create your own credentials. If you intend to become successful as a person or in the business world, you must first create a credible image of success. In the very beginning, when I was first starting to perform the seminars, Deborah was always in the back of the room shooting several rolls of film at every event. Whenever I traveled, I carried a loaded camera with me. There were always a variety of pictures to put in the newsletters and flyers. The pictures weren't about me; they were human-interest shots of the people who were interacting with me. Everything was always shot in a business setting. We were looking for action shots of me working with the seminar attendees. Although we didn't realize it at the time, those pictures were documenting our credibility.

All three of my corporations currently have their own Web site. Each site features hundreds of photographs of people attending my speeches and seminars. There's a navigation button on each site that links to a page called the photo album. Visitors to any of our Web sites can browse through dozens of thumbnail photographs. You'll also find recorded audio speeches I performed before live audiences as well as testimonial letters from our clients. Every page on every one of my Web sites has a lot of audio and visual credibility pumped into it.

A few words of advice to every new businessperson: Get testimonial letters from every client and take lots of photographs of your business. If you have employees, feature them in your newsletters. When photographing your business, use a lot of action photography instead of posed group pictures. Show your people interacting with the customers, using the machinery, working with each other. The object of these images is to create the impression of "bigness."

I still hire a professional photographer to come into my seminars and shoot several rolls of people shots. Every seminar registration form has a disclaimer and release just above the signature line at the bottom. When people sign up to attend my seminars they automatically sign a release giving my company the authority to use photographs of them in my advertising.

Every potential client who inquires about our services will receive a full presentation package on my company within twelve hours. Our company package is filled with testimonial letters, articles about me and the company, as well as reprints of articles I have written. They will also receive a video about the company and another video featuring excerpts from speeches I have performed. All of the testimonial letters are reproduced in the client's original letterhead colors to give our prospective customers a quality impression. Even in the start-up days when my company was new and money was tight, I would never send anyone black and white copy machine reproductions.

Be highly visible

Through the years, I have spoken at more than a hundred state, city, and national conventions as well as more than sixty automobile dealer 20-Group Meetings (mastermind groups) in various resort cities in several countries.

As a new company, or even as an established entity, you have to stay in front of your industry. I am still the foremost national columnist in a prestigious trade publication, *Dealer* magazine, and even though I am not paid to do it, I probably would pay them to let me do it.

Every month we mail thousands of flyers to past clients as well as to new prospects. We also send out a "fax blitz" to every customer in our database at least once a month. On any given day we have the ability to send more than five thousand out-bound faxes to subscription recipients. The strategy is to keep updated seminar information in front of our customers.

Our flyers are self-mailers, always on quality paper such as 60-pound white glossy stock and always in at least two colors, usually full color, with a photo on every folded section except the outer part where the stamps and the address go. Sometimes we mail three and four levels deep into the same company. We will usually send one flyer to the manager who is the actual prospect to attend the seminar and another copy to his or her immediate supervisor. We will also copy the owner of the company who is usually the decision maker. Most recently we've been sending a personal overnight letter to the owner of the company thanking him or her for inquiring about our services and urging him or her to visit our Web site. It is important that the owner is already familiar with your company and the benefits of doing business with you before their employees come to them with the flyer. If someone who receives the mailer is not interested, you have a better shot at landing the account with multiple mailers. By sending the flyers to several levels within the organization, you still have a chance a supervisor or even the business owner might overrule them and you'll still wind up with the business.

Fake it until you make it

Start doing prosperous things now. People are charismatically attracted to successful people. Often in my lectures I teach the principle "fake it until you make it." I have always believed that people are more likely to want to know you and do business with you if they perceive you are successful. People like hanging with successful people.

Here's an answer to an ancient paradox: The chicken most definitely did come before the egg. If you are ever going to become successful, you must appear to be successful already. You must dress like a success, you must look successful, and you must do successful things. You must hang around successful people and go to successful places. Drive a successful car and live in a successful place. Once you envision wealth and begin to act like you have already arrived, success and prosperity will happen automatically.

I encourage people to invest in their image. Somewhere out there I am certain there really is a barefoot kid with the purple hair who has this incredible billion-dollar dot.com company operating out of his parents' spare bedroom. I am sure that has really happened to somebody, somewhere, at some time or another. Realistically though, is this a business model you'd be willing to bank on?

Selecting a business

A unique business or is it just another dry cleaner? I sometimes catch myself laughing uncontrollably with tears streaming down my face when people tell me they're thinking about starting a new business in a low-income, high-failure industry. I assume you are looking to get into a business where you can make a lot of money and build a solid future for yourself and those people you care about. There are so many people who can't distinguish between a real profit-making business opportunity and their personal interests or hobbies. They dive in headfirst without looking and then get depressed because they aren't making any money. With today's technology, you have a wealth of research and information at your fingertips. It is available to virtually everyone.

What unique advantage will your business have over the potential competition? Are you thinking about a service or product people will pay for? What is it about your service or product that is so uniquely better than everyone else's similar products and services? If there is already a dry cleaner on nearly every street corner in your town, what makes you think your dry-cleaning business is going to succeed? If others have failed in the same type of business, maybe even in the same location, was it really because the previous owners were stupid? Do you believe your service and your advertising are going to be significantly better than theirs? Get real!

Most bankrupt businesses were destined to fail from the very beginning. It was obvious to everyone but the person who owned the business. Most business failures were predictable before they ever even opened the doors. I've seen so many people start ridiculous businesses based upon stupid concepts. Back in the early eighties there was a running skit on *Saturday Night Live* called "The Scotch Tape Boutique." It was about a couple that invested their entire life savings opening a store in a dying shopping mall. All they sold in the store was Scotch tape. Of course no business could ever hope to survive selling such a limited product line with such limited demand out of a store in a mall with no traffic. The only people who bought any tape were the other shop owners in the mall who needed it to post going-out-of-business signs in their windows. Is your dream business really just another Scotch tape boutique?

I am fairly sure there are a number of people who just threw this book across the room in a fit of anger. They are stomping around their living room right now, saying bad things about my ancestry. Unfortunately, they are the very people I was writing about in this chapter. They don't want to hear it. Many people are destined to fail and will ultimately ruin their lives because they are not willing to leverage other people's experience and expertise. As I have traveled all over the world, I have met many bankrupt hardheads with all of these great stories about how they almost made it.

Before you jump out there and invest in it, ask yourself whether your town or community really needs another landscape and gardening contractor.

I know so many people who have started their own business only to discover they have created nothing more than job replacement. They have become slaves who are shackled to a business with long hours and a low payout. Being stuck in a business you hate is far worse than being stuck in a job you hate. At least you can get fed up one day and quit your job. Once you've made a commitment to invest time and resources in a business, in most situations you just can't quit your business and walk away. You have got money invested and you've entered into contractual obligations, leases, and maybe even franchise agreements you can't get out of. It's hard to sell a business with poor cash flow. Once you are in it, the only way you can get out is bankruptcy. That's why so many people try and so many fail. Many people have ruined their lives because they selected the wrong business. It can certainly kill your spirit.

It takes money to make money

There's an old myth that says you have to be in business for a year, maybe longer, before you should expect to realize a profit. There are millions of people starting new businesses that are profitable from day one. Millions of people are becoming millionaires without a lot of startup capital.

Cash flow

I would never start a business if it couldn't generate immediate income. I have no interest in starting a business looking forward to some time in the future when it will eventually start to pay off my initial investment. I don't like to deal with inventory and product liability. As a consultant and as a professional speaker, my entire inventory is right here inside of my suit so-to-speak. The type of business I want is something you can start without employees and operate out of your home in the beginning. I would rather sell and perform services, than manufacture and warehouse products. What is most important, I am looking for a business with little to no receivable, a business where you get paid in full upon performance of the service.

You've got to be willing to risk money to make money

When Debbie and I started Supersystems on the kitchen table back in 1986, we had just enough cash on hand to last about six weeks based on our standard of living at that time. My wife and I had agreed that if the business wasn't profitable by the end of the first month, then I would give it up and go back to work and get myself a real job. Of course, I had credit lines to fall back on but it was our plan to be profitable from the outset. Actually, we didn't even touch those credit lines until the second or third year in business when we decided to grow the company.

Define your dream

The official party line in virtually every one of those how-to-start-your-own-business books or schools is that you need to have a formal business plan before you start a new business. I am sure that works for a lot of people, but I was a boot-strapper. I was one of those rare individuals who start up a new business totally undercapitalized, relying on guts and instinct. I intended to make a profit from day one and there were no contingent plans to borrow any money from anybody.

A formal business plan is for those educated, structured business types who need to present an idea to investors and bankers in a clearly quantified format designed for structured minds. My business plan was just a stack of yellow legal pads with all of my personal notes and thoughts. I viewed my business plan as something I wrote for myself, just for me, to get my thoughts organized into a clearly defined course of action. All I wanted from my original business plan was to get my thoughts on paper, where I could see my vision in print.

Identifying your customer's pain

When I started Supersystems, the entire idea was pure concept. There were no models to study because there were no independents doing hands-on sales and marketing consultation programs in the automobile industry. Having a lot of knowledge about the automobile business in Atlanta, I already knew which dealerships were successful and which were struggling. Having been a manager at several of the top dealerships, I also knew what types of problems even the best dealerships struggled with every day.

I've often heard it said you have to identify situations that cause your client pain, problems, and circumstances they struggle with. Find out what causes them to lose money or sales. Then design a business that offers the cure. One of the most profitable professions in the United States is the medical profession. Of course, the main reason doctors are able to become so wealthy is because people will pay anything to escape their discomfort. So will businesses.

Successful businesses satisfy a need. You have to show them your company can save them money or make them money, solve their problems, streamline their processes, or create harmony in the workplace.

Not all of your potential customers' businesses are broken. Sometimes the solution is simply to devise a way to improve the quality of their business. Maybe you just need to devise ways to cut their costs, improve their employees' morale, and increase their revenues.

Whether your company exists to solve problems or to create greater abundance for your clients, the wealthiest entrepreneurs in history have always been able to create their own markets where none existed before.

A home-based business is only the first stage, not the goal

This home-based business mystique is okay if you are simply content to reach a certain level and stay there. To me, a home-based business is just the first stage; it is not the end goal.

Home-based business enterprises just don't project the image of being a real business. I view most home-based businesses as job replacement. If the idea of becoming wealthy by operating a home-based business sounds like a dream to you, that's mainly because that's exactly what it is. True, many businesses start on the kitchen table but my theory has always been if a business is to become really successful, you must create an illusion of bigness a home office just can't create. Home-based businesses give your prospective clients the impression you are a small-time operation. Most companies and most individuals want to do business with companies they perceive to be capitalized and stable. People want to feel confident they're dealing with an experienced, professional company that will be around for a while. Home-based companies have an aura about them that says this isn't really a serious company. Everything about them feels temporary.

You never want to give your clients the impression you're operating on a shoestring, even if you are. Never, never use voicemail or an answering machine to answer your telephones. Whatever you do, never have your business telephone answered by your family members or children. The last thing in the world your customers need to hear is your kids or your mother-in-law answering your business phone. Even in the earliest days, when we were just starting out, a live operator answered our phone twenty-four hours a day. When Deborah was out, we transferred the phone over to our live answering service.

A home-based business will sound bigger and more professional when you hire the services of a full-time, twenty-four-hour live answering service. When customers call your business and get a recorded message, they get the impression you're a small-time operation. They might assume you're not reliable. If your business telephone is answered by an answering machine or voicemail, you might as well run a full-page ad telling your customers you're a small-time operation.

Let me just add another note here to show how some people think. Here is one of my pet peeves: When I call a company and the receptionist answers the phone with the words, "Hold please," and doesn't even speak to me, I will hang up immediately and make a mental note never to do business with that company.

I came to get the money

As I travel across the country speaking and consulting, there is one thing I never lose sight of. The reason I am out here is to get the money. I am a professional and I am worth the money I charge for my services. This is not my mission. It's not my calling. It's not my hobby. This is my profession. People are paying me for the years I have invested in learning my profession. They are paying me for the expertise in which I have invested hundreds of thousands of dollars to learn and develop. They are paying for the benefit of my experiences and the knowledge I will share with them. They are paying me to teach them what I know and to make their lives and their businesses better. I put my heart into the quality of my work and the services I provide for my clients.

If you can honestly say you have provided quality goods and services to your clients, you will never be ashamed to ask for the money they legitimately owe you. I never apologize for my fee and I am never embarrassed to ask, "Where's the check?"

Today I will be paid for my professional services

The ringing phone demands an answer. I roll over in the bed and start fumbling to find it. After all, I am not familiar with this room. I've survived thousands of hotel wake-up calls. Suddenly, I sit straight up in the bed, "Wait a minute! Where am I?" and the other question I ask myself is, "What am I supposed to be doing this morning?" and, "Am I late for whatever it is that I am supposed to be doing?" Every business traveler knows my story of how it all starts to blend together.

But one thing is the same: Every morning when I wake up in some strange hotel room—whether it's in Cedar Falls, Iowa, or Grand Cayman Island in the British West Indies—as I put on my tie, I look into the mirror and say, "Today, someone is going to pay for my professional services."

Do you remember the 1960s song *Homeward Bound* by Simon and Garfunkel? Those lyrics still haunt me. A small part of the price I have paid for my personal prosperity is the fact that, for the last fifteen years, I have found myself traveling more than 250 days a year, living in hotel rooms and airports, away from my family. I am often lonely and homesick. Even though my clients generally treat me like a celebrity, I am paying a hard price for my success.

Success often comes with a heavy price tag and the degree of success you wish to achieve will determine the weight of the payment. Remember in the early chapters when I challenged you about the depth of your personal commitment to succeed? I have seen so many people who said they wanted to achieve wealth and prosperity but they weren't prepared to pay the price. I am visualizing future rewards that will grow from the seeds I am planting today. The pain I experience today will create a better life for me and my family.

> As I put on my tie, I look in the mirror and I say to myself, "Somebody's gonna pay for this!"

You haven't made anything until you've been paid

In 1973, I started selling radio advertising for WVOJ, the number-one country radio station in the city. The owner and general manager of the radio station was a man named Dick Oldenburg. Opinionated and temperamental, Oldenburg ruled the station with an iron hand. He was a difficult man to deal with. There was only one way to do anything—the Oldenburg way. You could seldom reason with him or change his mind about anything. But the man was brilliant. His station was the number-one rated adult radio station in the city.

Oldenburg and I came from two different worlds. Then the worlds collided and here I was working for him. If it hadn't been for Jack Davis, the sales manager, it is quite possible Oldenburg and I might have killed each other.

In the radio and television advertising sales business, it is not uncommon for your customers to take more than sixty or even ninety days to pay an invoice. One of the policies at WVOJ was that the salespersons' commissions were paid upon collection, not when you sold the advertising but when it was collected and in-house.

Just to be sure the salespeople were participating in the station's cash flow, Oldenburg had set up a decreasing pay plan, based on when the money was collected. If a salesperson's client paid in advance, the commission was 35 percent; if they paid within thirty days, the commission was 30 percent; and so on. If one of your clients paid 120 days late, your commission dropped to 15 percent, and if it went to collection, you received nothing.

Not only was I developing and becoming a moderately great advertising salesman, I soon developed a reputation for being able to collect the money. I rarely had an account whose payment was running as much as thirty days late. There were salespeople at the station who actually quit over the pay plan. Even though they were able to sell the advertising, they were weak when it came to collecting.

Every day in my travels I meet businesspeople complaining about cash flow problems that are about to put them under. They have performed the work and delivered the merchandise and now they are waiting for their clients to get around to paying them. In most cases, these people have one quality in common: They are intimidated by the client and afraid of losing the business even though their big, powerful clients are floating their money.

The secret to getting the money starts when you get a firm agreement about payment from the very beginning of the relationship. I am never ashamed to approach the person at the highest level in any company and ask for the money when it is rightfully mine.

Occasionally, my employees still come to me to help them collect from those few accounts that owe us money. Believe me, very few people owe us any money. My accounts receivable is extremely light. But, there was an occasion when my wife came into my office with an old invoice that dated back more than 120 days. She told me the client's payable clerks were giving her the old runaround. They kept promising to send us the check and but it never arrived.

I knew I had given this particular client great value and now they were "mousing us" with our money. This is not the way I do business. I will bend over backward for a client but don't mess with my money. I looked at my wife standing there frustrated, with the invoice in her hand, and I said, "Okay. No problem! I'll handle it."

I really didn't want to lose this customer or their business, but I am always going to collect the money. Granted, the amount of money in this instance was fairly small, about 1,750 dollars. And, to make matters even more delicate, this particular client was also a consulting account, which represented about seventy-five thousand dollars a year in additional business. I knew they were good for the money. There wasn't any doubt in my mind they would pay eventually. This particular client was the type of account I would characterize as being *a little squirrelly* as opposed to being *a complete deadbeat*. Sitting there at my desk I immediately made a decision and, without hesitation, I fired off an e-mail to the president of the company. It read:

> Dear Tom (not his real name):
>
> My office is having some difficulty collecting on an old invoice for two of your employees who attended my December seminar. We've been in contact with Cindy in your payables department and I would appreciate it as a personal favor to me if you would look into it and expedite the payment.
>
> Thanks,
> Jim Ziegler

We had the check within three days, and even though I have seen him and spoken to him on the phone numerous times since, it has never been mentioned again. I am still doing business with his company, even though I am sure this is not the last time we will have to press them for payment.

The way my office is set up, collections are a priority and we get our agreements firm at the point of sale. Although I have never instituted the decreasing commission pay plan, my sales representatives today are paid commissions only upon collection, not at the point of sale. I look back on Dick Oldenburg with only the fondest memories and best wishes. It took me a long time to really understand and appreciate his business genius. The lessons I learned from Dick Oldenburg at WVOJ Radio nearly thirty years ago are still paying off every day.

One of the primary secrets to success in business is to have clear and firm agreements

I am not now, nor will I ever be, in the business of offering my clients credit or long-term billing. That's the primary reason our receivables have never been significant. The secret to getting the money is to set up your company with all of your priorities up-front, which includes an understanding with your clients that you expect to be paid immediately upon performance. I believe in firm agreements outlining your services and how you will be paid and when you will be paid. Right now, it is not uncommon for my companies to generate several hundred thousand dollars in a big month. Even though the overwhelming majority of our business is done without a formal contract—on a handshake, so-to-speak—we always get the money. The reason is simple: My agreements are clear and firm with no gray areas.

When we book a consulting visit or when we sell a seminar seat, we invoice the client twice, immediately by fax when the agreement is made and then again through hard mail with a copy of the letter of intent. I don't ordinarily use a contract unless it is an area where the other business will be paying me a commission. This usually occurs when we are selling their services or when we refer their company to a third-party client. The letter of intent details the terms of the relationship. The letter outlines when I will show up, right down to the airline and flight number. A letter of intent clearly delineates the responsibilities of both parties in the agreement.

A typical letter of intent might contain something to the effect that the client will arrange my hotel room to be billed directly to them in a Hilton-class or better hotel, or the client will provide transportation for me while I am in the area for this event, or the client will provide transportation reimbursement.

The letter clearly states that, upon presentation of invoice, on such and such a date, the client will pay directly to me a fee of a certain amount plus per diem of such and such an amount (including travel day) plus hotel, transportation, and first-class airfare reimbursement. The letter goes on to say I will be departing on flight number such and such, at this time, on this day. Notice the detail. Nothing is subject to interpretation. When I send a client a letter of intent, it specifies every part of the agreement in the smallest detail and defines every area of responsibility. It states my obligations to the client as well as everything the client is expected to do and what they are expected to pay and when. There is nothing that might be subject to interpretation or argument.

The second part of the letter not only outlines what services I will perform and what materials I will provide, it also stipulates that the client will instruct his or her employees to participate in our project with a spirit of cooperation. There have been many times through the years when it became necessary for me to shut a door and have a heart-to-heart conversation with my client. Many times I've had to point out their employees' lack of enthusiastic cooperation, which violates the spirit of our agreement. My agreements are so finely tuned that I am in control of the relationship.

Currently, my management seminars sell for 995 dollars per attendee for a two-day event. We offer a fifty-dollar, per-seat discount if the client pays in advance by credit card. We have the money in advance and it's in the bank. My seminars are always nonrefundable, unless there's a legitimate emergency. If a student doesn't make it to one of my paid-in-advance seminars, that client has a seat in the bank and they can send any employee to any future seminar. Once again, my agreements are clear and firm. I have collected the money for this event and there are no refunds except in the case of legitimate emergencies. This has been specifically outlined in my agreement with the client and there is no room for them to wiggle on the agreement.

The Prosperity
EQUATION

Advertising and Marketing and Sales...Oh My!

The nuts and bolts

Fasten your seat belts. We're now entering new territory. Up until now everything we've discussed has been philosophy and generalizations. This is the bonus. Everything you are about to read from this point forward is the icing on the cake. Through the years I've read a thousand books about how to become rich by starting a business. All of them focused on your thought processes but didn't spend any significant amount of time discussing specific techniques and word tracks. No matter what type of business you have in mind, there's got to be a quantifiable marketing strategy as well as a business philosophy.

The strategies I am going to describe in the following pages apply to all types of businesses, regardless of whether you are doing business-to-business applications or selling to the retail public.

If it is to be, it's up to me

Back in the early eighties I attended a seminar in Atlanta performed by the legendary Jackie B. Cooper. Jackie Cooper was the greatest sales trainer in the history of the retail automobile industry. It wasn't uncommon for a thousand paid students to be sitting at one of his events, hanging onto his every word. At one point in the seminar I attended, Jackie held the microphone close to his lips and whispered these words in a deep reverberating bass voice: "If it is to be, it's up to me."

I have built my corporate philosophy around the core meaning I filtered out of those words. Every one of my employees understands the concept and how it applies to their job description. If it needs to be done, then it is up to you to do it.

"If it is to be, it's up to me!" I have said those words to every job applicant. Recently I interviewed a woman for a position with Ziegler Dynamics as publicity director. This position is an integral part of my business plan over the next five years. She had an incredible resume and an advanced degree in her field. This is a highly paid, executive position. She was immaculately dressed, her hair and makeup were perfect. It was obvious to me she held herself in high esteem and was accustomed to an affluent lifestyle. I asked her a question I ask in every interview to every applicant. "Would you clean a toilet?"

She stared at me for a moment with a deer-caught-in-the-headlights look on her face. "What do you mean?" she asked.

"Would you clean a toilet?" I repeated.

"Well, yes, I suppose I would if I had to," she replied with an eyebrow raised and a quivering uncertainty in her voice. She was obviously confused as to where this heading.

You see, folks, my company only has five or six employees present on any given day. A while back, we were holding a seminar in our training room with more than fifty out-of-town attendees. As luck would have it, for some unknown reason, the cleaning service missed our offices the night before. We came into a mess left from the training session the day before. The seminar students would be arriving within the hour. Out of necessity, I found myself cleaning the men's restroom with a brush and cleanser. Every one of my employees chipped in emptying garbage cans and cleaning. In my company, your job description is whatever needs to be done.

When I set up my company, I put everyone on commission. Even my receptionist receives a handsome bonus each month based on seminar attendance. She is paid five dollars per seminar attendee on top of her salary. Some months that can be more than a thousand-dollar bonus. I had a sales contest last September and everyone who works in my little company, including the secretaries, got a large-screen television because we hit our sales goal.

When everyone in the organization is paid on sales, the attitude is electric. Everyone goes the extra mile to make it happen and nobody complains. There is an incredibly high level of enthusiasm when they answer the phones. I have been complimented thousands of times on my employees and their professionalism.

Gathering your customers' names and written permission to recontact them

Over the last fifteen years, there have been more than seventy-thousand people who have attended my seminars. Most of these people were managers and executives. Unfortunately, we lost touch with many of them because, early on in the development of my companies, we didn't keep an accurate database.

In the developmental stages of my business, we lost touch with some of our customers and seminar students when we misplaced their records or they moved away. This will never happen again. Today's employees are more likely to be transitional, on-the-move from job to job. Most employers no longer show loyalty to their people; therefore, their people are more likely to move on to other employment. I've been told it's a Generation X phenomenon. I have read that the current generation in the workforce does not have the loyalty or the work ethic of previous generations. Whatever the reason, most companies are struggling with high turnover.

Recognizing the fact that the people who attended our seminars today might evaporate tomorrow, we decided to devise ways to keep in touch with them after they have left their current employer. So now when we register people for seminars, our registration form includes their home address and phone number as well as their supervisor's name, their general manager's name, and the owner of the company's name. When we set up our database, we have the ability to send mail to attendees' homes as well as to their workplace. The reason we send the mailers to their home is because, if they change jobs, you still have ongoing contact with that seminar attendee. Another reason we mail to their residence, as well as to their workplace, is because, many times, a clerk or an office manager might mistake your literature for junk mail and the recipient may never receive it.

Many times a previous seminar attendee has changed jobs and ended up referring my company to their new employer because they received a flyer at home after they left their former employer. That's good business. I follow customers and prospects for life.

The other side of this coin is we still have the names of their immediate supervisors and the owners and officers of their previous employer on our mailing list so we can solicit them to send other employees or attend our events themselves.

In addition to the mail-outs, they will also receive regular fax updates and a monthly e-mail newsletter featuring every business offer and upcoming seminar.

There is a disclaimer on every one of our seminar registration forms every attendee must sign. The disclaimer is also a release authorizing my company to send them e-mail newsletters and fax transmissions. When they sign the disclaimer, it also allows us to use their photos, video, and voice recordings in our advertisements. This protects us if we use any of their photos from the seminars or if they were to inadvertently appear in any of our ads or promotional materials.

Anyone who requests to be removed from the e-mail newsletter list or from the fax queue is unsubscribed and taken off of the list immediately. We have the ability to send broadcast e-mail to thousands of people who have subscribed to our e-mail newsletters and advertising.

Database marketing for small business

What I am about to say to you is the most important business practice I will write about in this book. Today, as the retail-marketing consultant to several hundred small businesses, I encourage my clients to create a customer database. Your existing customers are always your best and least expensive sources of new business.

Why in the world would anyone even attempt to grow a business here at the dawn of the twenty-first century without the technology to manage his or her customer information? These programs are so cheap. Virtually anyone with a PC can manage their customer base as if they were a genius.

There are plenty of off-of-the-shelf, over-the-counter software applications capable of running and managing huge databases. In my companies, we use Goldmine to manage a client base of more than sixty-thousand names and situations. I know a lot of people who use Goldmine, or ACT by Symantec, or any one of a dozen other software contact management applications. They're all great.

We have been known to send out thousands of newsletters and flyers every month. It is important to feature a lot of pictures, articles, and human-interest items as well as industry news in your newsletters. My theory has always been to keep your information in front of the client and as many people in their organization as possible. I firmly believe some of my biggest deals were closed because I had cultivated friendships with secretaries, receptionists, and clerical people, the so-called little people many businessmen ignore. When I mail to a company, the mailing piece sometimes goes to three or four different people within that company.

If you don't have a database already, I suggest you start by buying a targeted mailing list. You can get the names on a disk or order the preprinted mailing labels. We use a company called Info USA out of Omaha, Nebraska. Regardless of which program you choose to organize your customer base, there are thousands of customized lists for sale on virtually any potential customer demographic that you might be targeting.

There is a company called Standard Rate and Data Service, which lists virtually every targeted mailing list and every e-mail subscription list you could possibly imagine. In other words, you can rent virtually any category of list you desire for direct mail marketing or mass e-mail marketing. Say your target market is women, twenty-five to thirty-five years of age who play tennis and live in residential communities with houses valued at more than a half million dollars located in the Midwest. You can actually refine such a list by merging several other lists. There is no targeted demographic conceivable you couldn't put together a mailing list for. Standard Rate and Data Service is online at www.srds.com.

When we are putting together a flyer for our Prosperity Seminars, we buy targeted mailing lists aimed at *opportunity seekers*. Everyone on the mailing list is someone who lives in our target geographic area who has inquired about business opportunities or subscribed to entrepreneurial magazines.

When we are targeting our marketing aimed at a specific professional group, we first contact their associations and organizations. Most professional organizations will sell you their membership mailing list. It's relatively simple to get the information you need to build an effective database. The secret to keeping past clients is not only superior customer service; it is also dependent upon your ability to keep a high-profile presence with them. This requires frequent and effective customer re-contact.

In short, I have to know every means of recontacting every customer we've ever done business with, forever, in every way they can be recontacted. I want their address, their work phone number, their home phone number, their cell phone number, their pager number, their e-mail address, and their fax number.

A database should be a two-way conversation with built-in feedback from the customers to you. If I were in a business dealing directly with the public, I'd devise ways to get my existing customers to register with me. Why do you think so many of the large department stores are always trying to get you to sign up for a free gift or a drawing?

As a retail consultant, I am constantly getting my clients to capture the names of their customers through newsletters, contests, drawings, discount clubs, and preferred customer cards. If you seriously want to enjoy increased future business from your existing customers, you need to build an up-to-date, working database. I've advised many of my consulting clients to create an elite class of customer with special discounts and privileges. The Delta Airlines Platinum Medallion Program is a good example.

If you've ever done business with General Nutrition Center, you know they have an elite program for preferred customers complete with a GNC Gold Card. Those with the card get a 20 percent discount on purchases made on the first Tuesday of every month.

A few years ago my wife and I visited Santa Fe, New Mexico. One of the highlights of the trip was our visit to a cooking school taught by a famous regional chef who was an expert on preparing southwestern cuisine. Of course my wife had credit card in hand buying cookbooks, spices, and cookware associated with the adjoining shop. Two years later, we are still receiving mailers and advertisements, Christmas cards, and invitations from those people. That's great marketing. Of course, if I owned that business, I would have already added an interactive Web site capable of taking credit card orders as well as a monthly newsletter to their marketing strategy.

Capture the names, addresses, phone numbers, e-mail addresses, buying habits, and purchase patterns of your customers—such as when they bought last, how much they spent, what they bought, and the names of the members of their family. Create custom fields and filters in your contact management programs to be able to refine your mailers to zip codes, states, type of customers, customer preferences, and service intervals.

Publish monthly newsletters

It is important to keep your information in front of the client or the prospect and as many people in all levels of their organization as possible. The number of repetitive impressions each customer receives and registers is the true measure of all advertising effectiveness. That is why most businesses need to produce a monthly newsletter.

It is imperative for you to keep your name in front of past customers without the in-your-face directness of an advertising piece. In other words, newsletters are less likely to turn someone off than a hard-sell direct mail piece. Newsletters are friendly and folksy. They seem to float around and are frequently passed from reader to reader. The advertising message in the newsletters is subdued and more subliminal. They are a great way to reach out and capture new customers.

Every business needs to have a monthly mailed newsletter as well as an electronic monthly newsletter.

The first newsletter we produced back in 1986 was a two-page, single-folded mailing piece with a stamp on the outside. Self-mailers not only save the cost of envelopes, they also help ensure your piece is read. We mailed that first newsletter to more than three hundred business owners in the state using a mailing list we borrowed from another company. It was like we had struck gold. Suddenly, for the first time, people from out of town were actually driving to my seminars and staying overnight in hotels.

Newsletters drive the business

In those early startup years, our monthly newsletter was by far the single-most powerful thing we did to drive the business.

Since then, my articles in magazines and the newsletters have continually elevated the company image and enabled us to prevail over the competition.

Creating a newsletter does several things. First, it gives the reader the impression you are an expert with something to say. Second, it keeps you in front of clients and potential clients and it gets them talking about you. The more controversial the stance you take, the more debate you will generate. No matter how small a startup company might be, a newsletter should be one of your first projects. Pictures equal credibility; therefore, newsletters should contain a lot of photography. Photography humanizes your business, especially if your potential clients recognize some of the people in the photographs. They may recognize the names of some of the other successful companies you are working with when they read your newsletter.

Every customer recontact via a newsletter should offer them some personal value. The subliminal message says your company cares about them beyond the value of the money they spend. My newsletters have always contained human-interest stories, testimonials from our readers' friends and neighbors, and sometimes, from their competitors. Occasionally, the newsletters have even featured Mom's cookie recipes.

An electronic newsletter

As of right now, the Internet is still wild and free. I suspect the government is plotting to find ways to tax Internet usage. An article I read recently sent chills up and down my spine. It seems several members of the U.S. Congress are planning to introduce a bill creating e-mail postage. They are planning to charge five cents for every e-mail sent. It will be a horrible day for millions of entrepreneurs when it finally passes. But, if it happens, we'll still find new and innovative ways to do business.

Today, right now, as I write these words, e-mail is still free. One push of the button sends out thousands of letters to thousands of people. All of these messages arrive semi-instantly to every recipient. Why in the world would any businessperson in their right mind not be sending out a regular e-mail newsletter? The software is inexpensive. As a matter-of-fact, you can do it directly out of Goldmine, or Act, or any of your mail-pro programs.

I need to add one important footnote here. All of your e-mail newsletter recipients must be subscribers who registered with you and asked to be on the e-mail newsletter list. There must also be an easy way for them to unsubscribe from your e-mail list and be removed from future mailings.

100 telephone contacts a day

On those rare occasions when I am actually in the office, I have been known to make as many as one hundred phone contacts in a single day, calling previous customers, prospective clients, managers and employees, personal friends as well as industry contacts. I am regularly in close contact with all of those people who make up my circle of influence. The idea is to keep my name out there, to stay fresh in their minds. There are so many people I have known who were flying high, on top of the world, and then they woke up one day only to realize they're out of touch and they've become Old News.

Project management

Most of the self-made wealthy and successful people I have known have one common characteristic. Almost without exception, these people seem to have the ability to manage multiple projects simultaneously. In life and business, it seems to me the winners are always going to be those people who can keep the most balls in the air.

You're never going to have an effective network of friends and associates unless you've developed superior contact management skills and superior personal organization. Believe me, we're talking about work ethic and discipline here. Using modern technology, I have the ability to remember people's names, their spouses' names, their children's names, their birthdays, when their children graduate from high school, their anniversaries, and virtually anything else I have picked up from them in previous conversations.

Instead of concentrating all of my public relations efforts on the decision makers, I make it a point to learn the names of their relatives and employees as well. When a secretary or spouse answers the phone, I always call them by name: "Hello, Pat. This is Jim Ziegler. Is Donny available?"

I can tell you about their hobbies and what their dreams are. I remember exactly what we spoke about last time we had a conversation. I never miss an appointment or fail to return a call. I'm never ever late for an appointment or a meeting. Never.

The reason I am able to juggle so many projects so successfully is because I make generous notes about everything important that pops up over the course of these conversations. I know exactly what we spoke about and exactly what I promised them and exactly when I promised to recontact them. Whether it is a client, a personal friend, or one of my seminar attendees, I have a record of every conversation, contact, and business dealing we've had from the beginning of the relationship.

Your personal memory is incapable of keeping up with all of this information. It is impossible for one person to stay on top of all of these projects without a technology-based system. The most successful people in life and business stay on top of all of their ongoing projects. I am talking about everything and everybody. To become successful, and ultimately prosperous, you must learn to master project management technology. I use an off-the-shelf software application called Goldmine.

Telephone blitz

A telephone blitz is much more than just a bunch of random sales calls. When I am on one of these telephone blitzes, before I pick up the phone, I always review the data on the computer screen in front of me. I want to get a fresh picture in my mind of what we last spoke about. I review any notes I might have made about their business or events in their personal life. I also review any contacts they've had with our company, what conversations they've had with my employees, and what products or services they've ordered in the past.

First of all, I know exactly when I last spoke to them, it's on the screen in front of me. For instance, if they told me their son was getting married in April (and it is now June), I might ask how the wedding went. Of course, as you may have already guessed, their son received at the very least a card—maybe even a gift—from me. I know their son's name and use his name when I inquire about him. An excerpt from my side of a typical telephone conversation might sound something like this.

"You and Fred have been married for twenty-five years? Really? When's your anniversary?...November 12. That's next week.... Yeah, you sure got that right! I'll be married fifteen years next month. Oh, boy! I am really glad you reminded me, I almost forgot about it. My anniversary is December 8. How could I forget? It's the day after Pearl Harbor Day."

When she told me her anniversary was November 12, I immediately made a note of it in the database. Of course, they will receive a card from me every year from now on. My computer is programmed to always remind me of every important event in my clients' lives.

If they said they want me to call them back on a certain day about a certain subject, they will receive a call at the exact time I said I would call and I will remember exactly what we discussed last time we spoke. I program into the computer what I call reminder flags to pop up in and remind me about the appointment and what the agenda is. You can set an alarm in the program to remind you about any type of call or appointment.

"Hello, John. Jim Ziegler. If you'll remember we spoke back on October 15 about sending some of your managers to my seminar in Atlanta and you asked me to call you back sometime in the first week of December. As I recall you were thinking about sending John Jenkins and April Thomas.... Let's go ahead and do it.... Okay great, I'll get my people to set up their travel arrangements with them. By the way, last time we spoke, you and Cindy were getting ready to go to Europe for your anniversary...How was the trip?"

Sometimes, I am able to use their own words from a previous conversation to remind them how much our relationship has benefitted them. "Susan, last time we spoke back in April, you told me your production was up 30 percent after your managers returned from my seminar and started using some of the techniques they picked up. Would you mind sending me a testimonial letter about the successes you've had using my programs?"

Telephone touches

When I am blitzing through my database sometimes I'm just trying to make a lot of short, soft customer contacts. Nothing substantial…just saying hello. Most of these calls last less than two minutes. (Unless I get a bite, that is.) The idea is to talk to as many customers as I can every day, every week, every month. These are just low-pressure, casual conversations. They usually start out something like this:

"Hey, Jennifer. James Ziegler. I just called up to see how your business is doing. Truthfully, I don't have an agenda for this call. I just wanted to follow up with you to let you know I hadn't forgotten about you. Have you been getting my newsletter?…

"Are my people doing a good job handling your account?… Great! By the way have you checked out our new Web site?… You like it? Honestly, I didn't know that. Fantastic, thank you very much. We did a lot of work on it.… Yes, I'm very proud of it! Thanks. Well, I just wanted to say hello and see if there is anything I can do for you.… Okay, you did? Now that's incredible! I am really excited to hear you got the deal. I know you've been chasing that one for a long time.… Okay, great! Look, you've got my number if you need me. Even though I'm traveling, you know I return all of my calls promptly. Listen, Jennifer, sincerely, thanks for your business. I'll call back soon."

That's it! The fact I just called her without making a sales pitch of any kind was appreciated and will be remembered by the client. Notice, right in the very beginning of the conversation, I announced this wasn't a sales call. Of course, I can't tell you how many of these calls actually do result in sales because the client asks a sales question.

Notice, I always speak with a client in a personal way. This is how it becomes a relationship and not just another account. There is a passion and an enthusiasm in the tone of my voice they can pick up on the other end of the conversation. Don't you hate it when someone calls you with a dull, monotone, disinterested tone of voice? It certainly doesn't give you the impression they are sincere. So many people speak on the phone as if it were only an exercise in common courtesy. They are just going through the motions. You don't get the feeling they actually care. Energy is contagious. When I told my client I was glad they got the contract, there's no doubt in my mind they knew I was sincere. They heard it in my voice and they felt it in their heart. There's a powerful Anthony Robbins philosophy I have tried to incorporate into every sales presentation. Tony describes it as selling with passion.

You must find a way to carve out the time, no matter how busy your schedule is. These customer recontacts are too important. I travel more than 250 days-a-year while I am running a business with six employees and seven-digit annual revenues. I have to have focus and a strong work ethic.

As I type these very words, I am at the Luxor Hotel in Las Vegas where I have just finished a big seminar. As soon as the seminar was over, I ate lunch and came back up here to my suite and sat down at the computer. It takes a lot of discipline to be successful. I have found the most successful people are those who have the ability to manage their projects with precision. You must eliminate wasted time.

Technology changed all the rules

We're living in some very exciting times. In today's arena, David can slay Goliath by operating a low-overhead business. You have technology available that will allow you to perform multiple tasks simultaneously. Just a little over a decade ago, most of these projects would have required a staff of ten or twelve people to accomplish.

We now have the ability to be in touch as we travel. Cellular telephone technology puts everyone in contact and allows you to communicate and do business while you are mobile. When I had my first car phone installed back in 1986, I can remember how radical everyone thought it was. In those days my bill was running upwards of twelve hundred dollars a month.

It boggles the mind when I think of what might have been. Back in the early 1970s when I was selling radio advertising, I drove all over the city calling on clients and had to stop to find a telephone at least a dozen times a day. Even if we could have comprehended the concept of cellular technology back then, we would have thought it was something out of *The Jetsons* cartoon show on television. How much more productive would my sales day have been if I had the freedom of mobile communications twenty years earlier?

Shortly after I arrived in Atlanta in 1982, I attended my first automobile finance school which was sponsored by General Motors Acceptance Corporation. That was the first time I actually used facsimile technology. Many of the car dealerships in those days were still using "quip" machines, which had the ability to send a facsimile document over the telephone lines in about three minutes. Now, less than twenty years later, we have the ability to send paperless fax documents directly from computer to computer at incredible speeds.

Another giant advance in technology we often overlook is the fact we now have the technology to put our materials, documents, and information in our customer's hands immediately. It's absolutely amazing.

We have the ability to ship materials to destinations virtually anywhere in the world. Even if they are thousands of miles away, I can have a package sitting on their desk tomorrow morning. I am talking about putting videos and packages and promotional materials in my clients' hands by ten o'clock, next-day delivery. That wasn't even possible ten years ago. In the 1980s, if you sent your client a letter or package on Friday, it might be delivered by next Thursday.

Ten years ago, the pace of business was comparatively slow and constipated. Invariably, you always ended up losing your momentum. There was no such thing as a surprise attack. If you were trying to take an account away from a competitor, they always found out about it before you were able to sew up the deal. They had time to counterattack your strategy while your materials were in transit. Today's technology gives you the ability to take an account away from a competitor with stealth precision. By the time they realize you're doing it, it's already over.

E-mail and electronic document transmission over the Internet allow me to communicate with literally thousands of people at the very micro-moment I left-click the mouse. Just put the cursor over the "send" icon and click. I can send absolutely flawless documents in full color in a matter of microseconds. Instead of waiting days for the U.S. Postal Service to deliver my literature to a prospective customer, I can sit there on the telephone as we review my Web site together.

The Internet, fax machines, cellular telephones, e-mail, personal computers, all of these incredible new technologies give the small business entrepreneur the ability to create and compete. This is real power.

Embrace technology

In my experience, if a business doesn't have a Web presence, the reason is usually because someone at the top level is afraid of new technology. I am talking about the owners, the managers, or the decision makers. I call this disease Technophobia. I have seen many companies fall off of the edge of the earth and disappear into the abyss because the powers that be were intimidated by technology.

You are not computer literate. You don't understand the Internet and all of this new technology, and it scares you to death.

Well, folks, the truth is that you need to get involved with the Internet as a focal hub of your marketing strategy.

I am extremely technologically challenged. I don't have programming expertise and I don't know how to write code and I don't know how to build a Web site. If the truth be known, sometimes I have difficulty loading new programs into the computer. You don't have to know how to do any of these things to operate a computer or to make a Web site produce business. Using the same logic, I do not know how to repair a car but I certainly know how to drive one.

Then embrace change

People instinctively resist change. I believe it's part of a greater defense mechanism that lies deep within all of us. In the business world, if you resist and try to ignore all of the rapid-fire technological changes being thrown at us, you will become roadkill on the information highway.

Then learn new skills

I regularly sign up for one-day classes at the neighborhood technical college on how to use the different programs we are using in our business. Today, as the president of the company, it would be perfectly acceptable, and none of my employees would question it, if I were to choose not to learn how to use these programs. That's what I pay them to do. Even so, I have signed up to take some advanced classes later this month on how to use the Goldmine program.

This wasn't something that came to me naturally. In the beginning, when they first put a computer on my desk, I had to force myself to sit down and come to grips with my anxiety about the technology. I was going to have to face and conquer my fears and uncertainties. Throughout the day, when I am actually at my office, I have to call one of my staff into my office at least three times a day to show me how to do something with one of the latest programs.

Some of the people who really know me think it's incredible that I am traveling around the country speaking to business groups and chamber of commerce seminars about how to increase your business through Internet marketing. I am recognized as an expert on the subject. In December of 1999 I was actually interviewed on CNNfn as an expert on business trends into the new millennium.

You see, I readily admit I don't have the expertise in the technology. My expertise is in the application of the technology. I can't build a Web site but I know how to make a Web site sell and produce business. There are technical people available to me who can physically perform the things I need to produce the results I describe to them.

Internet marketing strategy

Let's talk about first things first. The good domain names are disappearing fast. It's important to get your Web site registered and lock in your business address on the Internet as soon as possible. Even if you don't plan to actually build your Web site until some time in the future, register the domain name now. It doesn't cost much and, like I said, the good names are being grabbed up. The most prestigious dot.com designations are rapidly becoming unavailable.

You can check to see if a domain name is still available by going to www.register.com. If it is available, you can immediately register it with a credit card. This is just one of the many ways to register a Web site. I have registered more than seven domain names, although I am currently operating only three Web sites. I will figure out what to do with those other names as new business ideas hit me.

Something everyone should do immediately is register their own name. You might think that would be a no-brainer, but I'd be willing to bet most entrepreneurs haven't got around to doing it yet. A few months ago, my Web guy asked me if I had registered my own name as a domain name. Of course, I hadn't. I always figured there was plenty of time to take care of that, so I was constantly procrastinating and putting it off. Well, you can guess what happened. There was already a Web address for www.JamesZiegler.com. That blew me away. Some guy in California had already registered the name James Ziegler. Now I started to panic as we checked out alternative choices. I was finally able to register www.JamesAZiegler.com and right now I am just trying to figure out exactly what kind of Web site I will build using my own name or if I just want to use it as another portal to one of my existing sites.

A Web site is supposed to be a marketing tool

The problem with most Web sites is they are usually built and designed by nerds! I have nothing against them. Some of my best friends are nerds. Allegedly, the wealthiest human being on the planet is a nerd. It is difficult to run a business today without employing their services. My Web guy has become one of my closest friends.

Notice I didn't call him my Web "master." There's something about that term that just doesn't sit too well with me. Especially when the so-called master shows up in my office with a sweatshirt still sporting yesterday's mustard stains, shorts, and flip-flops. That term "master" sounds like something to describe the powerful evil sorcerer in some Dungeon and Dragons game. I prefer to say Web guy. It just fits.

Unfortunately, nerds are not usually marketing geniuses. They are technical people and they think in linear thought patterns. Nerds usually don't make great salepeople. When you are designing your Web site, listen carefully to the advice your Web guy—or gal—suggests, but don't forget to think about marketing. For instance, most techies will tell you not to put a lot of pictures and graphics on your Web site. They say the site will take too long to load up and your visitors will lose patience waiting for the site to load, and go elsewhere. They think that way because that is exactly what they'd do personally. I disagree.

If you ever have the opportunity to visit my Web site at www.ZieglerDynamics.com, you will notice the home page resembles a pinball machine. There are flashing titles and a ton of photographs and little dancing images with directions for the visitor to "click here." Being a marketing guy, it is inevitable that my ideas will usually conflict with the Web guy. My Web sites all have a lot of motion directing the person where I want them to go and flashing signs directing them to what I want them to look at. My Web sites even speak to you in RealAudio, narrating what the visitor is looking at on some of the pages.

Directing traffic

The problem with most business Web sites is obvious. These magnificent billboards are built on the dead-end side streets of the information highway. Nobody ever goes there. They are never seen. A Web site is worthless unless you have the ability to direct traffic to it.

Although my company operates several multimedia Web sites, I don't look at the Web sites as sales producers as much as I consider them to be extensions of our advertising message. ZieglerSupersystems.com and ZieglerDynamics.com are, for the most part, corporate information sites. I have other Web sites aimed at the retail public, as well as business-to-business Web sites, which are aimed at my business clients and prospects. Most of the visitors showing up at our Web sites didn't just stumble onto them while they were surfing across the Web; we directed them to go there.

Unless you are Rip Van Winkle, and you just woke up from a twenty-year sleep, I am going to assume you have used search engines to navigate and find things on the Internet. Even though it is extremely important to have your site registered with the search engines, you are still going to have to use other marketing strategies to drive traffic to your Web site. Search engines are no longer the most effective way to get qualified visitors to your Web site. There can still only be ten names in the first ten results of any search. Everybody already knows all of the same tricks you do to manipulate the search results. We've all studied the same techniques to get our sites among the top ten. There are still only ten in the top ten. Even if you do manage to manipulate the search engines to get your site to come up in the first ten results, you will probably be knocked out of the top ten the very next week by somebody else who is now playing the game better. There are more effective ways to get qualified prospects to visit your Web site.

All marketing revolves around your Web site

According to the Federal Trade Commission, there will be more than 100 million Americans on the Internet before the ink is dry on the first printing of this book. I wouldn't even dream of trying to put a time or number on it in these pages because the statistics are exploding. It is growing faster than you are able to quantify it. Let's just say it's a really big number. This sucker is growing at an incredible speed.

In my seminars, I always ask the audience how many have an e-mail address. In some audiences, as many as 78 percent of the attendees were using e-mail on a daily basis.

Building an opt-in, voluntary, subscriber-only e-mail list is the cheapest and most effective way to advertise ever devised. As I've mentioned previously, you can reach virtually hundreds of thousands of people instantly. Currently, we have the ability to send unlimited messages worldwide at nearly the speed of electricity.

Please note that I am talking about sending subscription-only e-mail, not unsolicited, unwelcome junk e-mail—"spam" in Web jargon.

Your Web site is the hub of all of your advertising. Every other medium drives the customers to your Web site. There are two things I expect my Web site to accomplish: it must have the ability to gather information and it must inspire the customer to act immediately.

Not just selling machines, my Web sites are like so many additional pages of newspaper advertising. Every business card, every newspaper ad, every mailer, every flyer, every piece of company letterhead, every television commercial and every radio spot, every customer contact, and every advertising piece I send out is designed to get the customer to visit my Web site. My ads might read: "For three pages of additional specials and sales prices, visit our Web site at www.ZieglerDynamics.com."

Some of my smaller clients simply place little one-inch classified ads in a lot of different newspapers using reverse print, black background with white ink. Their advertising message might say something like, "Bargain Vacation Packages! Visit www.CheapTravelDestinations.com." (That is an unregistered, fictitious Web site address as of this writing.) When the people see those tiny, double-reversed ads, it directs them to visit the Web site, where they will see twenty interactive pages of additional information. These tiny ads expand a small inexpensive message into many pages. My small clients now have the ability to compete with the big companies with those giant advertising budgets. We are effectively turning small classifieds into the equivalent of many full-page, display print ads. Hopefully, their Web site has the ability to get the customers visiting the site to register for a contest or drawing so they can capture the name and address of the visitor, as well as send them automatic e-mail follow-up letters, by subscription.

Every television commercial should have big flashing print across the bottom of the screen directing viewers to visit your Web site now for twenty pages of additional sale items. Your newspaper ads and flyers should have huge borders directing them to your Web site address for more pages of specials.

Your Web site must be multisensory

When a prospect enters one of my Web sites, they are greeted by a voice message in RealAudio that says, "Enter the Incredible World of Ziegler Dynamics." Your Web site should have a lot of color, motion, and imagination. You also need to have technology on your Web site to direct the customer to register onsite with a program called an Auto-Responder. An Auto-Responder is a program that automatically sends sales follow-up letters to prospects who register with your Web site. The moment they complete the form on the Web page requesting more information, the Auto-Responder will automatically send them a follow-up letter via e-mail. This happens immediately, while they are still on the Web site. Most people visiting a Web site when they are at home are probably using the only telephone line in their house. They may not have the ability to pick up a phone and call you right now. Chances are, if they leave the Web site and move on, they probably won't remember where they saw the information. That is why it is important to get them registered while they're still a hot prospect. The automatic letter they receive via the Auto-Responder puts a copy on file in their computer. Then the Auto-Responder continues to send them a series of sales follow-up letters every day for a week. Statistically, most customers require repeated impressions before they will make a decision to act. A series of progressive follow-up letters increases your closing ratios dramatically.

128

Right now, the technology is available to put video and audio on your Web site. Your Web site's visitors can watch PowerPoint slide shows while listening to voice-narrated tours of your company or presentations of your products. A real estate broker can feature three-dimensional guided tours of your model homes, complete with voice-over narration. You can advertise sale prices and specials. Your Web site can feature your restaurant's menu and take reservations online. You can even send them a confirmation or a two-for-one coupon directly through the Auto-Responder.

Your Web site must be able to perform automated marketing processes

If you want your Web site to sell products, you must have an ordering page with the ability to take credit card orders automatically over a secure Internet connection. I would also give the customer the option to fill out and fax back a form, just in case they don't feel comfortable putting their card numbers on the Internet. Always give the customer the option to send a check or money order to an address as well. Maybe you want them to e-mail a survey back to your list server. It would also be smart to offer a toll-free, twenty-four-hour method of ordering as well. Make shopping cart technology available for your customers to order everything directly off your site. This is as important for business-to-business applications as it is for retail businesses.

ZieglerSuperSystems.com is currently selling somewhere around fifteen to twenty thousand dollars a month in supplies to our consulting clients. We are currently setting up special, nonpublic Web sites that will allow our business-to-business clients to order training items, supplies, and forms online, twenty-four hours a day.

Once a customer has responded and signed up with the Auto-Responder on the site, an automatic list server maintains your e-mail database and sends follow-up letters or a series of newsletters. Research has proven that a progressive series of four, five, or even six follow-up letters is substantially more effective than just sending one letter. All of these functions are done automatically, at preprogrammed intervals, strongly reinforcing the selling message.

These automatic follow-up letters are not junk e-mail, or spam, because your customer has actually requested more information and even subscribed to the newsletters when they signed up on the Web page and registered with the Auto-Responder.

All e-mail follow-ups, even though customer-authorized, need to feature an easy way for the consumer to "unsubscribe" and be immediately taken off of any automatic mailing list. I don't want anyone to receive my messages and newsletters if they don't want to see them.

There should be a dedicated person (or persons) in your company whose responsibility it is to sweep your site hourly throughout the business day, responding promptly to all inquiries. If your business is to be centered on Web commerce, you must develop a seamless strategy for shipping and confirming orders.

As your company grows, you'll need to consider incorporating a business development center into your marketing plan. A business development center is a central location where all of the incoming and outbound customer contact telephone calls are handled. More than just some kind of a boiler room, it is the technology center of your company. The business development center processes all customer requests, orders, and recontacts as well as follow-up.

Tear the sucker down and rebuild it once a month

Would you read the same copy of a *Time* magazine over and over again if you were given a choice? Most of us would rather move on and read something fresh and new. No offense intended, *Time* is a great magazine but I would become bored silly after reading the same issue over and over a couple of times. The same holds true of your Web site. People are not likely to keep revisiting the same site if they're only going to be seeing the same old tired stuff they saw last time. Once you've built your Web site, consider it as part of your ongoing advertising budget, not as a one-time expense. Change your Web site as often as you change your newspaper ads. Tear the sucker down, redesign it, and rebuild it regularly.

Give your customers a reason to return to your Web site. How many reasons can you invent to inspire them to revisit your site repeatedly? Always offer new information, new articles, new photos, and new layout and design. One of the greatest attractions to a Web site is something for free—contests, recipes, information, products, discounts, and coupons just for registering for your newsletter or for filling out the information on your Auto-Responder. They need a reason to register and to come back often.

Is your Web site a psychologically powerful selling machine, or just another brochure? Unfortunately, many Web sites seem to be growing cobwebs. They've become ghost towns on the information highway.

Advertising, sales, and marketing

Whether you're starting a new business or looking for ways to grow an existing business, your immediate focus should be maximizing sales and profits. This part of the Prosperity Equation focuses on how to generate new customers as well how to stay on top of repeat business. You can master advertising, marketing, and promotions even if your business is operating on a limited budget.

In 1908, legendary retailer, John Wanamaker said, "I know that half of my advertising is wasted…I just don't know which half."

In 1988, James Ziegler said, "I do!"

John Wanamaker did not have the technology to pinpoint the effectiveness of his advertising nor did he have the diversity of media today's businessperson is dealing with.

With today's technology, there's no excuse for wasting your advertising dollars.

I've often heard it said that you cannot control those things you cannot measure. We have the tools available to pinpoint the effectiveness and the results we get from every dollar we spend.

Why advertising is tuned out

I submit to you the reason most advertising doesn't work is because the consumers have tuned it out. There are so many messages coming at them from so many different directions, it is little wonder no one pays attention or even consciously hears the messages anymore.

From cradle to grave, the average person is bombarded with advertising and frankly, most of us are experiencing more than a little inner rage and rebellion. In recent years we've seen a conscious consumer backlash against all advertising messages.

Why most advertising has become just so much static in the background of your life

Most advertising is what we call push marketing. This is when the advertiser forcibly intrudes into the consumer's private space and tries to take center stage. It's sort of like when you rent a movie and discover there's ten minutes of unwanted advertisements at the beginning of the tape. Unfortunately, we can't fast forward past most of the other advertising that is being thrown at us. Most sales and advertising today is offensive, trying to push the consumer into a decision they weren't even thinking about.

Picture this: Your phone rings. It's another telemarketer who "just needs a minute of your time." We've all felt rage and indignation when our personal privacy is invaded by messages and unsolicited sales pitches. We've had it up to here with all of this advertising coming at us from virtually every conceivable direction. Is it any wonder that all of your potential customers have tuned it out?

Today's advertising is delivered in subtle ways. The hero in the movie is drinking a Pepsi. Every piece of clothing you wear has the label and the logo in big letters, on the outside of the garment for all to see.

Your potential retail customers have become desensitized. They're not paying attention anymore. It's no longer just enough to put a message out there, you have to be able to stand apart from the crowd, cut through the clutter, and inspire your prospects to take action.

I have studied advertising and promotions most of my adult life. One of the reasons I was able to set sales records in Jacksonville when I was selling radio advertising was because I was selling the results instead of just selling spots. My clients trusted me to create concepts that worked.

Now that you've made the decision to become an entrepreneur, you need to become aware of advertising and promotions. When I first decided to become a student of my industry, I learned to analyze every ad. If one of my competitors had a successful sale or promotion going, I studied every facet of their campaign.

Once again, listening to the experts, I've watched dozens of videos and listened to hundreds of tapes on marketing and advertising. Over the last thirty years, it wouldn't be an exaggeration to say I've read thousands of books and magazines on the subject. I prefer to study the maverick marketeers as opposed to the more traditional Madison Avenue agency types. Some of my contemporary marketing heroes are people like Jay Abraham, Dan Kennedy, Ron Popeil, Jay Conrad Levinson, Corey Rudl, and Don LePre.

Listening to Jay Abraham helped me to expand my imagination and how to write hard-hitting headlines that work.

Dan Kennedy is famous for his direct advertising strategies and the incredible results he is able to achieve with sales letters.

Ron Popeil is a marketing legend. If he isn't the father of the infomercial, he certainly is the master of the genre. I am the proud owner of one of Ron's rotisserie ovens and, I've got to tell you, it's a great product too!

Jay Conrad Levinson is the guy who authored all of those great books on *Guerilla Marketing.*

Corey Rudl is the supreme Internet marketing guru for startup entrepreneurs.

And, of course, then there's Don LePre. I don't know why, I just love this guy. Strictly from a marketing viewpoint, he is a study of the art of schlock. I don't find Don offensive or obnoxious in any way. He's my kind of guy. Don just wants to teach you how to be rich just by placing these tiny little ads in thousands of papers. You know what? I ordered his course a few years ago, and there's a lot of value there.

Through the years I have invested at least a hundred thousand dollars buying tapes and videos by entrepreneurs and motivators like Don LePre and Tony Robbins. I buy tape libraries and some of the products offered just so I can study what these people are doing. From strictly a business perspective, I study what others are selling successfully. In other words, if it appears to be successful, learn how they're doing it.

I must own every how-to-do-anything course and all of the tape sets that were ever sold to anyone by anybody. I never thought of any of it as a waste of time or money. This is just investing in my future business.

If you are planning to start a business selling directly to the retail public, you must be prepared to study retail marketing. The traditional media of radio, television, and newspapers can swallow an amateur advertising budget faster than a Vegas slot machine. Each of these advertising venues requires some specialized techniques and strategies to create promotions that result in sales. There are unique psychologies involved in structuring ads that sell.

Every Saturday morning I love watching the parade of infomercial personalities. What we are actually seeing here is some of the best there is in immediate-response advertising you will see anywhere in the world. You can learn a lot from these programs if you carefully study the psychology packed into every word and demonstration. Susan Powter is outrageous as she struts and sells ways to make you thin and healthy. George Foreman is selling the newer, bigger, better, improved Lean Mean Grilling Machine. I love all of these people. They have become like close personal friends. My all-time favorite is still Mike Levy. You know who he is, the nerdy little guy in the argyle sweater and black-framed plastic glasses. He gets so excited about the juice machine or the bread-maker. That kind of excitement and enthusiasm sells products. When you watch him sell, it's like watching a little puppy that is so excited you know it's about to pee all over the place at almost any second. I love it!

The Home Shopping Network has a limited supply of genuine Diamonique tennis bracelets. You need to get a move on and call now! Operators are waiting! The timer in the bottom of the screen is counting down. You've only got three more minutes before our limited supply runs out and this offer is gone forever…or until next week, whichever comes first. This is the absolute epitome of urgency and limited supply advertising.

Sally Struthers cries and pleads and begs you to help her feed starving children all over the world. This is a classic example of what I call guilt-complex advertising

The outside of the envelope says you've just won ten million dollars from Ed McMahon or Dick Clark. By now most of us have caught on that we probably haven't won anything yet. Still, a shot at a million bucks or more is a great incentive to open the envelope.

Every Web site you visit has banners and hyperlinks designed to lure you away to other Web sites where you honestly didn't want to go to in the first place.

More uninvited, intrusive advertising appears in your e-mail. You've even got a very personal e-mail message from a lady you've never met named Stormy who is inviting you to visit her personal Web site if you'd like to see her private pictures. This is the new-age version of "Hey, sailor, looking for a good time?"

An immediate call to action response

To grow and to become increasingly more profitable, you must devise ways to stand apart from the crowd. Your message has to fight its way to the front of the line. Let's talk about some techniques to cut through all of the defensive filters and barriers your target audience has put up to screen you out. Not only must you be able to make people pay attention to your advertising message, you've got to make the message reach out and grab them by the throat. Your advertising must be able to shake them up, excite them and motivate them to take action. It is abso-

lutely imperative to get them to act now while they are still under the ether of the buying emotion. There's got to be a hook in
the message to motivate them to act on those impulses immediately while the feeling is still warm and alive. All advertising
must create an immediate call-to-action response.

When your advertising demands an immediate call to action
response from your customers, your company must be awake
twenty-four hours a day to service the business while customers are in the heat of the buying emotion. The odds are
overwhelmingly against customers recontacting you if they cannot reach you immediately. That is why your business has to
have a twenty-four-hour toll-free number, especially if you are
advertising out of your area. If you are selling to the retail public, and even in most business-to-business applications, you must
have the ability to receive immediate payment by credit card.

A unique selling position

All sales presentations and advertising should address the
unique benefits of the products or services you are offering. Your
unique selling proposal is something about your product or service they won't find elsewhere, at this price, of this quality, in
this much quantity, that is this easy to operate, or comes with
this guarantee.

Other than price, you have to identify what is it about your
offer that will be uniquely important to your customer. What is
your unique selling position? That is the main ingredient in this
soup. Your unique selling proposal determines the measure of
your competitive advantage.

Sadly enough, when I am involved in corporate sales training, it's obvious that most salespeople can't define why their
product or service is a better value than the competition's product or service. When you can't quantify the superior value of
your products and services then cheap prices are your only option.

In most of my sales training sessions, I ask the attendees to
tell me, in detail, ten reasons why a customer would buy my

product or service instead of the competition's products and services? Try that with your own situation and see if you can come up with ten concrete, believable reasons?

All advertising messages must hammer home what it is that separates you from the competition. In other words, what do you do that they don't? What do you offer that they won't? Why is your product or service better than theirs?

Large corporations advertise and little guys promote

What I really love about *The Guerilla Marketing* books by Levinson is that they are aimed at the "little" guy or gal. Whether you are starting a brand-new business or whether you are the president and CEO of an old-line established corporation, I am going to assume the majority of business people who might be reading this book haven't got millions of expendable dollars to experiment with your advertising. If you are not Burger King or Budweiser or General Motors, you can't afford to speculate as to whether or not your advertising is working. You haven't got the money or the time to chase bad ideas if these ideas aren't working and producing immediate results. Your advertising has got to generate immediate and measurable results.

Institutional advertising and generic advertising just don't make sense for most small businesses. Those high-dollar advertising campaigns are for the big guys. The rest of us have to practice specifically targeted advertising aimed directly at those people who are most likely to buy what we're selling. Brand-name and image advertising are for the large corporations with mammoth budgets.

Even though I have worked with many Fortune 500 companies, the majority of my business still comes from smaller businesses. My best customers are the small, entrepreneurial businesses, family-owned businesses, franchisees, and local service businesses.

I am a believer in promotional advertising. Two-thirds of the word "promotion" is the word "motion." When I see the word promotion, I break it down into the two words that most readily come to mind: professional motion. In the context of advertising to small businesses you need to build your advertising around an event.

Unlike John Wanamaker, the small players have to be able to measure the effectiveness of every advertising dollar that we spend. All advertising has to result in increased sales and profits.

Every dollar spent in advertising must generate a net profit return of twenty dollars

Entrepreneurs and small businesses need to develop a total marketing strategy; a plan where every dollar spent translates into immediate and measurable increases in your profitability. We can't throw money at bad ideas if those concepts aren't working. Most entrepreneurs make the mistake of falling in love with their advertising whether it is working or not. No matter how much you've become attached to an ad or a commercial, the bottom line is the only measurement. Is it effective? Can you see concrete, measurable, profitable results? You haven't got the time or the budget to be experimenting with marketing concepts if they don't produce immediate sales. A small business' advertising and marketing plan must realize a high closing ratio of sales as a percentage of opportunities to do business. If an advertising campaign only produces high volume traffic, a lot of new friends who never buy anything, then your budget is wasted.

I believe your marketing is supposed to be a proactive process—high-energy, high-response, high-impact, in-your-face advertising. When I design an advertising campaign, it has to be demographically targeted at those people who are statistically most likely to buy what you sell or do.

I can't emphasize enough that your advertising must prompt the customer to take immediate action. Targeted marketing involves feedback and response management. There has to be a built-in follow-up and a customer recontact mechanism. This goes back to information management. All businesses must maintain an active customer database. A small business must design your advertising strategy with the end objective of gathering the names and addresses and phone numbers of your customers—and their permission to recontact them.

More than just advertising, marketing is a total concept involving every facet of the process that brings your customer and your product or service together. Advertising is only a part of marketing.

> "Any business without an organized and measurable sales process is like a lost puppy in the middle of the interstate during five o'clock rush hour."

Marketing actually starts with the physical sales process, how you present your product or service to the customer, the price, the method of payment, the display, and most importantly, what you and your employees do and say when you are interacting with your customers. You've got to have good sales techniques and great presentations and great support materials. Your employees need specific training on product presentation, including word tracks and sales techniques, or the competition is going to run over you.

Death of a Salesman

I have seen the stage play *Death of a Salesman* by Arthur Miller perhaps twenty times. It is magnificent. Starting in the 1950s with the version starring Broderick Crawford, I've also seen it performed by Lee J. Cobb, Jason Robards, Ralph Waite, Hal Holbrook, Judd Hirsch, Brian Dennehy, and even Dustin Hoffman.

Having been a professional salesman since I was eight years old, I often think we are the most misunderstood animals on the planet. Those poor souls who were never fortunate enough to have ever been a salesperson just don't get it. Salespeople are goal-driven and competitive. We are a very special society, a fraternity or sorority of adventurers. Salespeople are often maligned and slandered because we live and die based on what we produce, rather than taking money for simply showing up. We are those brave souls who passed up the civil service job with the post office because we preferred to be paid what we are worth. Commissioned salespeople are paid for the strength of their personality and their ability to persuade others to see it their way.

Death of a Salesman is about those struggles and conflicts. Even though it appears that he died a failure, Willy Loman personified the entrepreneurial spirit. Personality sells!

In one scene a neighbor observes, "Willy is a man out there in the blue, riding on a smile and a shoeshine. And when they start not smiling back, that's an earthquake."

Nothing on Earth could be closer to the truth. When they start to stop smiling back, that is an earthquake.

In one classic scene in *Death of a Salesman*, Willy turns to his son Biff and says, "A salesman has got to dream, boy! It comes with the territory."

Your corporate personality

You see, Willy Loman did have the right idea. Your company's marketing vision begins when you create a corporate culture and a corporate personality. People will not do business with you simply because they like you. But if there is one thing you can be sure of it's this, they will never do business with you if they dislike you, or in this case, if they don't like your company. You better have a dream, a corporate vision, a concept of who you are, and a defined image you want to present to your potential customers.

Every company must have a creed, a philosophy, and a mission statement that all of your employees buy into and your customers feel every time they do business with you. In my own companies, I legislate likability. In other words, it's not optional. My employees are pleasant and personable at all times; it's part of their job description.

No amount of advertising and marketing can overcome bad service or surly employees. Today's consumer will not tolerate an unfriendly customer environment. An old adage in sales says, "You have to touch their hearts before you touch their wallets."

Own your customers for life

Most businesses could not tell you who their customers are. They haven't a clue as to where they live or how to reach them. Their customers are completely anonymous. They don't know how to recontact them. They've never studied or quantified their preferences or buying habits. Most businesses do not know how to effectively reach their customers or how to re-advertise directly to them. They don't know when or why their customers stopped doing business with them or how to get them to come back.

Using an efficient database system for business-to-business sales and marketing, I have the ability to keep ahead of the competition while, at the same time, making indelible impressions upon my customers. In my companies, I have the unique situation where I find myself doing business with both the general public as well as business-to-business sales and marketing.

When a company is starting up or when a small growing company is starting to expand, the efficiency of your sales and marketing returns are crucial. In other words, it is absolutely necessary you realize a high closing ratio and the best results from your efforts. You don't have the time or budget to experiment with marketing concepts. All marketing efforts must produce sales.

Look for gold by mining your existing customer base

Let's take a second here and examine how to market services to another business.

First of all, identify your market. Exactly what type of client is your prime target? Who is most likely to buy your services? How do you get a list of these prospects?

I assume you have a database management system. Most businesses are so busy prospecting and advertising for new customers that they neglect their old customers. Directing all of their advertising resources into inviting strangers to do business with their company, they've become so focused upon charging straight-ahead, barreling headlong into tomorrow, that they've lost sight of what made them successful in the past. I will tell you unequivocally that your existing and past customers are your best and cheapest source of future business.

Are we spending so much time looking for new business that we've forgotten to service or recontact our existing customers?

The most important marketing strategy I discuss in this book applies to virtually every business in the world: *Capture your customers for life.*

When I started my first company on the kitchen table in 1986, I had a very simple philosophy, "Once you've captured a customer, never lose them." Years later I stumbled across a book by Carl Sewell titled *Customers for Life*. This is must reading for the serious business owner.

As a business consultant, when I first become involved with any business, the very first project is to set up their database. All other forms of marketing are diminished unless they have the ability to recontact all of their existing customers.

My wife and I are regulars at a little sandwich shop not far from our offices. We probably eat there six or seven times a month. The elderly man who owns the sandwich shop knows us by sight. We've been coming there for so long he even knows what we are going to order before we ask. Like I said, we've been regulars there for years. Recently, however, it occurred to me he doesn't even know my name or my wife's name. In reality, he doesn't know anything about me. If we ever stopped coming in, he would probably be acutely aware we were missing. "The nice couple who used to come here several times a week haven't been back lately." He certainly wouldn't have any way to contact us or to find out why he lost our business. If we just suddenly stopped coming in, he'd miss us but he could never find us again. We'd just be gone.

If you've ever seen my photograph, you may have noticed my hairstyle is not exactly a work of art. Obviously I don't spend thousands of dollars trying to create a hair styling masterpiece. I am a balding guy and I'm fairly comfortable about that. I usually get a haircut wherever I happen to be when I need a haircut and whenever I have the time. About three years ago I was sitting in the waiting area of a little neighborhood haircut shop in Snellville, Georgia, where my son often has his hair cut. This shop is part of a franchise with more than a hundred locations nationwide.

As coincidence would have it, the president of the entire company just happened to be there, in that particular shop, on that particular day. When Zach and I checked in at the reception desk, the woman asked me if we had ever had our hair cut there before. I said my son had and she asked me for my telephone number. I realized she was pulling our information up in their database.

While Zach was getting his hair cut, I sat in the reception area waiting my turn. Naturally, it wasn't long before I had struck up a conversation with the franchiser. This is the guy who founded this company. He sells the franchise rights to the operators of every location nationwide.

We got into discussing what I do for a living and then, somewhere in the conversation, I asked him this question, "What kind of customer follow-up do you do out of your database?"

He was very proud of their incredible customer-tracking software. He told me the managers usually picked three or four names at random each day and called the people at home and surveyed them about the quality of their experience. These random customer satisfaction surveys were 100 percent of their in-person, customer recontact strategy. They occasionally used the database to mail out coupons and special promotions.

That's when I hit him right between the eyes with the most important question I ever ask any businessperson, "Can your database identify when a customer has stopped doing business with you?"

For a moment he just sat there with a puzzled look on his face. I'd seen that look before. I knew he couldn't answer that question. Frankly, it had never occurred to him.

I continued. "It seems to me that the average haircut client should take somewhere around six weeks between visits."

I had his undivided attention now. After all, this is some good stuff. It was obvious he wanted to hear more. He sat there listening intently, making some notes on an envelope.

I went on. "If one of your customers hasn't had a haircut in sixty days, will your computer notify you when they are missing? Will some type of alarm or a flag or a reminder window jump up on your computer screen and inform you when this specific customer hasn't been back in your shop for sixty days? How do you find out what's wrong, why they haven't returned, and what you need to do to save the business? You have no contingency plan to recapture a lost customer before they are lost forever."

Even the simplest contact management program allows any business to preprogram a reminder every sixty days, or for any other time period you choose. What if you were to put a sixty-day reminder notice or an alarm into the computer every time the customer came back in? Of course, when they came back sooner than sixty days, you'd simply move the reminder another sixty days into the future. When they didn't show up for sixty days the reminder would pop up and you would have identified a potentially lost customer. Why in the world would any restaurant or hair salon or any type of recurring service business for that matter not use such simple technology tools to track their repeat business? When I find out one of my customers is missing, I go looking for them. They cost too much to replace.

The lifetime value of a single customer

Let's assume a barbershop's average customer spends about twelve dollars per visit. Now, let's pretend the customer revisits the shop every six weeks. If the average American family lives in their immediate neighborhood for an average of seven years, the value of losing one of the barber's average customers is about 725 dollars over the lifetime of their business relationship. If it's a family we're talking about with several small children who are also getting haircuts, the lifetime value of the business just went up to twenty-two to twenty-three hundred dollars.

Repeat business from existing, past customers is cheaper than soliciting new business from strangers

You cannot view your customers as a single, one-time transaction. No business can afford to allow a single customer to stop doing business with it without making an all-out effort to keep them.

What does it cost to get a new customer and what can you afford to give them to stay with you? Could you imagine a restaurant spending their advertising budget to get a customer through the door and then having him or her eat there only one time? Of course not—the value of a customer is repeat business. Once they arrive, the main reason you want to dazzle them with superior service is because you need priceless word-of-mouth advertising, which compounds the value of your original advertising as well as the repeat business.

Can your restaurant afford to spend as much as a hundred dollars in advertising to get each new customer through your doors for a fifty-dollar meal? The only way that would even begin to make sense is if you can be statistically certain they will continue to come back, at least twice a month, for the seven-year average they will probably live in the neighborhood. The lifetime value of each customer's business justifies the higher cost of quality advertising. The intangible multiples of increased business through good word-of-mouth advertising increase the value of a single customer. This is true in retail, sales-to-the-public businesses, as well as business-to-business sales applications. I am willing to spend a lot more to get a new customer because I have calculated the lifetime repeat value of their business.

A basic philosophy in keeping customers for life is to be able to identify exactly when customers stop doing business with you. If you can find out why they left, then you can invent ways to recapture their business immediately before they form other loyalties.

Recently, while watching late-night television, I heard that the average American has an immediate circle of influence of about 250 persons. Truthfully, I don't know where that number came from, or if it's even valid, but let's pretend for just a moment that it's an accurate statistic.

An angry customer has the mathematical power to become a nightmare. While we're still in the pretend mode here, let's also suppose one of your angry customers has told half of the people he or she knows about a bad experience with your company. Now, let's imagine those people telling only half of the people they know about the bad things they'd heard about your company. Now, repeating third-hand, embellished information, those people tell the story to only 10 percent of the people they know.

Congratulations. You've just potentially blown out 406,376 customers. That could equal the population of a small country. And now, theoretically, they all hate you.

Of course, that is humorous and exaggerated but it does hammer home the point. In reality, any amount of bad word-of-mouth is devastating, especially since most of the people who hear it probably live within a couple of miles of where you do business. One customer badmouthing your company becomes an infection. The reason you go to extremes to satisfy them is not to get their business back. I would usually be just as happy if they never came back. The reason I want to go overboard to make them happy, at any cost, is to shut them up. Great word-of-mouth won't always necessarily grow your business but bad word-of-mouth will always kill you.

Harvard Business School revisited

Back in the eighties, Mark H. McCormack wrote several books on the subjects, *What They Don't Teach You at Harvard Business School* and *What They Still Don't Teach You at Harvard Business School*. In both of these bestsellers, McCormack's complaint about the shortcomings of Harvard Business School, or any other business school for that matter, was that they were teaching business history. Our advanced institutions are turning out executives whose expertise centers on the way things have always been done in the past.

McCormack's philosophies revolved around entrepreneurial skills, sales, and marketing. The skills and techniques he discusses in these books are usually "the school of hard knocks," insights that most of us picked up on the streets, learning as we went along. Reading these books will certainly shorten the learning curve for many new business people. I consider McCormack's books part of my advanced education in the school of real life in the real world of business.

Although I have never met McCormack, there is no doubt in my mind he would probably agree with me that "there's nothing on Earth you can't sell your way out of!"

How to grow your business once it starts rolling

If you're not growing, you're dying. In my experience there is no such thing as the status quo in business. You can't just get to a certain level and then start treading water and expect to remain at the level at which you've arrived. The only way to stay in business is to grow.

It's a war out there

Now you've arrived and your business is percolating, you might be tempted to lie back and relax a little. This is when many business people might start to become complacent and fall asleep at the switch. Regardless of what type of business you have, you can be absolutely certain of one thing, someone out there is planning to take it all away from you. Every day your customers are being seduced away by a competitor, or worse yet by "the new kid on the block," some little startup business that is leaner and meaner and hungrier than you are. The way your company used to be before you got fat.

It never ceases to amaze me how many businesses operate without a growth strategy. It's as if these people show up every day without a plan, just reacting to the day's events. They're in a fight but they're only throwing counterpunches. Most of the businesses that go under never saw it coming. By the time they realized they were losing it, it was too late. There's always someone in the rearview mirror looking to pass. What if W. T. Grant had taken K-Mart a little more seriously? What if Sears and J.C. Penney had paid more attention to Sam Walton's little startup operation and reacted sooner? Remember when the first wave of Japanese automobiles caught the American manufacturers snoozing back in the seventies? They were all so stuck in their smug "we're the big dog and this is the way we've always done it" paradigm they nearly lost everything.

How many old-line, established, bricks and mortar corporations have suddenly awakened to find they are fighting for their very existence? The big guys are under siege by an army of new technology entrepreneurs and e-commerce competitors.

Most businesses reach a point where they are just going through the motions. They just continue to open their doors every day, doing what they've always done, but the truth is they will not keep getting what they've always gotten. Doing what you've always done is one of the quickest ways to lose your business. If you're not continually innovating new concepts and looking for better ways of doing business, then you're dying. So many business people are running scared, afraid of the competition, facing each new day just hoping they can dodge enough bullets to make a profit. They are so busy reacting to the competition that they spend very little time thinking about new and innovative ways to grow their business. They're all so busy trying to stay where they are without sliding backward, they forget the objective is to try to get to the next level.

Increase your sales volume

There are many ways to grow an existing business. The most obvious way is to sell more of your products or services. Increasing sales volume is the most immediate action you can take to stop the bleeding when your business is not profitable. Logically, it's the first strategy most businesses embrace in their marketing plan. Although it's obviously your first option, it's not always the most profitable option for the more farsighted business plan. With increased sales, there is always an increased cost of doing business. There are always additional production costs, commissions, and salaries, as well as the need for new equipment, more employees, and more advertising. Higher sales volume often requires additional space, storage, and locations.

Increase the amount of profit per sale

A more immediate way to grow a business is by increasing the amount of profit you make on each sale of your products or services. By increasing the profit produced on every sale and new transaction, you maximize the amount of revenue each sale generates. There are several ways to accomplish this.

The most obvious way to increase the amount of profit per sale is by raising your prices. If your business is such a unique, one-of-a-kind, got-to have-it, can't-live-without-it, can't-get-it-anywhere-else kind of product or service, then maybe you can get away with that tactic. Most of us, however, are running businesses in a competitive environment and you can only raise your prices so often before it starts to run your customers off. Most businesses have a threshold where sales become price sensitive.

A more rational approach to increasing profits per sale is to find peripheral sales of other products and accessories that are of interest to your target customer. You can sell more products and other services to the same customer as an adjunct to each sale.

This works in retail, direct-to-the-public, as well as in business-to-business sales and marketing applications.

One of my personal marketing heroes is George Zimmer at the Men's Wearhouse. Zimmer's marketing approach is honest and straightforward. I love it when George turns to the camera and points right at you, smiles, and says, "You're going to look good in your clothes, I guarantee it!"

The honesty and sincerity his commercials project literally jumps out of the television screen and grabs me by the throat, shakes me up, and drags me all the way down the street to the mall. I love the man's confidence and his relaxed delivery. He's genuine, honest, and believable. The message is powerful.

I buy all of my suits there. Maybe I like to do business with the Men's Wearhouse because I admire good salespersonship. I have done business with at least four different locations of Men's Wearhouse, and they are all a consistent, class act. They are genuinely interested in their customers and it shows. I have got to believe that is the culture George sought to create when he started the company. This image is obviously carefully crafted and orchestrated from the top down. Employees are aware of their mission statement and they live it. It didn't happen by accident.

At the Men's Wearhouse, once you've selected a new suit, while you are still in the dressing room, several employees are setting up a display featuring your new suit surrounded by an array of color-coordinated accessories. An assortment of matching ties, socks, suspenders, shoes, shirts, belts, and cufflinks are laid out with your new suit. There's no hard sell here. There doesn't have to be. When people are buying new suits and wardrobe they are excited because they know they'll be looking good in their new clothes. After all, George guaranteed it! When they lay out all of these beautiful accessories that perfectly match the clothes you're buying, emotions kick in, you're going to be excited, and you're going to buy something. You just can't help yourself—I guarantee it!

Whenever I shop at The Men's Wearhouse, I always end up buying additional stuff from them. This is what I am talking about when I say increase the amount of profit per transaction.

Incredible customer service

Although he probably doesn't realize it, another one of my personal marketing heroes is a man named Bruce Arnett who owns Carnett's Carwashes in Gwinnett County, Georgia, right in my own neighborhood. I've known Bruce for more than ten years now.

I met Bruce Arnett as a result of a nasty letter I wrote to him back in 1990. I was severely upset about something or another that had happened when I was dealing with his carwash. Truthfully, I haven't the foggiest idea of what happened to get me so upset; but I was really ticked off at the time.

Bruce tried to call me several times at home and at the office but I wouldn't take his calls. He wrote me a letter and I refused to respond. Then one day, he just showed up at my office demanding to see me. This guy cared about a single lost customer enough to drive thirty miles across town to my offices in the middle of his workday to apologize and do whatever it took to make it right.

Bruce Arnett definitely realizes the lifetime value of just one single customer. Most businesses would have written me off. Certainly, very few businessmen would have taken the time and made the effort to rescue a single lost customer. Bruce Arnett is a very successful businessman and his time is valuable. Nevertheless, he doggedly and relentlessly pursued me until he recaptured my business. Now, that's incredible customer service. I have done business with Carnett's Carwashes for more than a decade now, and there isn't even a thread of a possibility that I would allow anyone else to touch my cars.

I always get the Ultimate Carwash, which is their best service. It is more than thirty dollars per visit, if I don't buy any auto accessories or personal items. Sometimes, I have my car done three or four times in a single month. My wife has her BMW washed there several times a month, and I even trust them to wash and wax my vintage Corvette. In addition, I always tip the people out front. We are great customers and that's the way they treat us. But, I've discovered that's how they treat everyone. Bruce Arnett must have come from the same school I did. It's obvious he realizes your past customers are your best and cheapest source of new business.

From the moment you hit the drive you realize this is not your ordinary, run-of-the-mill, everyday kind of carwash. Like Bruce himself, Carnett's is a class act. The young woman approaches the car and calls me by name. I would prefer to think she knows my name because I am such a big shot, because I am such an important customer, but then I realized she also called the very next customer by their name. I watched her for a minute and I saw what she was doing. Carnett's Carwash has a database that lists my car's license number. She had already pulled up my account. She knew my name and my history before I even got out of the car.

"Will you be having the Ultimate Wash again, Mr. Ziegler?" she asks. "We have a special on the Shine Express Service this week. Want to hear about it?" All of these people are friendly and enthusiastic. On the walls are framed articles from newspapers and magazines about the Arnett family and their contributions to our community. This is a high-energy place. It just makes you feel good being there. You genuinely get the feeling they are glad you're here.

Walking up the ramp into the building you can't help but notice how spotless the place is. All of the employees are well-dressed, in uniform shorts, baseball caps, and tops. The cashier knows me; she's been there a long time. There's something good about doing business with familiar people. She reminds me this is my eighth wash, just two more trips before I earn a free one.

I had just bought a new Cadillac Escalade and was still heavily under the new car ether. I always have a special honeymoon period with every new car I buy. I was browsing through the gifts and accessories in the Carnett's boutique while I was waiting for my car to be washed. Most carwashes make some sort of feeble attempt to sell a couple of aftermarket items with little, tacky pegboard displays located near the cash register. This is different! Carnett's has this really big, well-lit, extremely nice boutique area with everything from the traditional car scents and accessories to greeting cards.

Although I wasn't particularly in the market for any new car accessories that day, I am the easiest sale in the universe to close. We're talking about a world-class impulse buyer, with references. Let's face it, a professional salesman like me is an easy target for a sale.

There it was, hanging on the wall just above the air freshener display, a custom chrome tag with a raised gold Cadillac emblem. I knew it would look great on the front of my new car. Of course, you already know the rest of the story. Before I could take another breath, I was frothing at the mouth, eyes glazed over, with a credit card in my hand. I bought that beautiful chrome and gold plate for the Escalade, which amounted to an additional seventy-five dollars, over and above the price of the carwash.

These principles work for all types of businesses regardless of whether it's a retail business selling directly to the public as in these examples or whether it's a business-to-business sales and marketing application. I have both types of sales in my companies.

Get your existing customers to do business with you more often

Once your business has maximized the profit opportunity of every single transaction, the next logical step in the process of growing your business is to increase the frequency of the sales with the same customers. In other words, you need to get the same customers to come back to you and buy more often. At Men's Wearhouse, for example, whenever you buy a suit or pair of slacks there, the salesperson always invites you to bring your clothes back anytime between cleanings and they'll press them for free. That's brilliant! Not only is it great customer service, it also ensures that your valued customer will return often and get into the habit of visiting your store.

Another good example of this concept is automobile leasing. About fifteen years ago the manufacturers started realizing most of their customers were keeping their old cars longer between trade-ins. The main reason people weren't trading cars as frequently was long-term financing and the fact that quality was improving. Cars were better built, so they lasted longer. As cars became more expensive through the years, people began financing longer so they could afford the payments. With the proliferation of sixty-month automobile loans—and even some seventy-two and eighty-four month loans—becoming available, average consumers found themselves owing too much money on the car to be able to trade it in when they wanted to. So, as a result, people were hanging onto their cars until they paid down the loans sufficiently to be able to trade.

That's when the manufacturers stepped in and came up with the idea of short-term consumer leasing. Short-term leases were designed to shorten the trade cycle. Leasing not only offered lower payments but now their customers could drive the cars for just two or three years and then trade them in or simply give them back and get a new one. As a bonus, they now had more, late model, clean used cars to sell. Leasing allowed auto dealers to sell more new cars to the same people more often. They increased the frequency of the transaction.

In my own business, we were looking for ways to sell more seminar seats to the same people. We sell our seminars to individuals as well as to businesses. Some of the biggest profit seminars are the training seminars for sales managers and finance managers in the automobile industry. Sometimes these seminars will gross as much as a hundred thousand dollars over a four-day event. We have thousands of graduates in our database.

It's always been my policy that, once you've paid for any seminar title, you may reattend that seminar at no charge, for life. They never have to pay again once they have attended any of the seminars. That keeps them coming back once or twice a year, and they usually convince their employer to send someone else with them who is attending for the first time, at full price. When I am performing out-of-town events, we always contract the hotels on a sliding scale. The more attendees who stay at the hotel at our group rate, the lower my meeting costs. If enough people stay at the hotels in my room block, the meeting space is free. There have been many months when the no-charge repeats staying at the hotels saved me thousands in meeting costs.

Recently, we decided to have a big sale in the seminar business. This is the first time I've ever tried this type of promotion.

154

Anyone who has attended either the sales manager seminar or the finance manager seminar at any time in the past could attend the other seminar at half price during the month of October. The sale was an overwhelming success. Ordinarily, sales managers and finance managers don't cross-train, but the sale on the attendance has created an atmosphere that makes the offer difficult to refuse.

Bigness has no boundaries

I don't know about you, but I would probably have been more than a little disappointed if God had decided to build a small, finite universe. My universe is limitless and the opportunities are endless. There are no walls around your imagination either.

I've never met anyone who could pinpoint the exact place where the universe starts or where it ends. It is fair to say that it is bigger than we can fathom. All you can do to describe is sort of to say, "Wow! This is really one heck of a big place we're all living in here!" You have no concept or comparison or words with which to measure it.

I am planning some incredible big things right now. I am working on projects that are so large they will make some "small thinkers" scream out loud and shudder in disbelief. But then again, I often find myself running with the big dogs. Sometimes I find myself associating with people who are operating on a higher level. In these circles, my giant dreams are considered to be "small thinking." Big fish in small ponds never grow.

Right now I am planning to hold Prosperity Seminars in cities worldwide, with audiences numbering into the thousands. I can already see these events clearly in my mind. Right now, the only thing holding me back is the details. That's the way everything in life is. It's all about the details, isn't it?

Well, this is my final challenge to you. Do you have a dream unfulfilled? Could it possibly be that the only thing standing in the way of your success and prosperity, maybe even standing in the way of your happiness, is just "the details"?

We've all heard the saying, "No guts, no glory." If you haven't got the guts to go for it now, then just when do you imagine it is going to happen? I have repeatedly given you the combination to the vault. What more can I say?

Follow that dream

Elvis had a movie back in the sixties titled *Follow That Dream*. I have heard some great speakers build an entire presentation around those words. As I write the last part of a book that has taken me more than a year to finish, it occurs to me the next one will be a lot easier to write. All of us have so much to do and so much to say.

In these pages, I have tried to quantify the basic ingredients in the recipe I used to cook up my personal success. As I have pointed out repeatedly, my way isn't the only way to get there. It might not even be the best way. All I can say is this is what worked for me and many other people to whom I have taught these principles.

From the mind-set to the journey, all of the way through the philosophies, to the specific techniques and strategies, this book transitioned four times.

In the very beginning, I laid down the Prosperity Equation broken down into its four cornerstone elements as well as the fine-tuned peripheral components required to realize the highest levels of success.

Secondly, I asked you to take a naked look at yourself with your defenses down, with no excuses. We talked about focus, mind-set, and philosophy. I challenged you to make a commitment.

Also, I told you my own story in a way I hoped would illustrate the principles of the book in your mind. I wanted to inspire you with a vivid and colorful personal painting called *Unlimited Possibilities*.

Finally, I discussed the specifics of starting, owning, and operating a business, marketing and advertising, and sales.

Admittedly, I threw a lot at you in a compressed format. Remember, most of the Equation is in your head. It's an attitude and philosophy thing more than it is a technique thing.

I rarely find the time to completely finish reading a book all the way to the last page. Usually, by the time I am halfway through, I start to catch myself skimming over the pages and jumping around from chapter to chapter. Considering the fact you're still here and still reading this is extremely gratifying. I am honored we have managed to stick it out together. Yeah, I know I might have insulted you way back in the beginning but it was a calculated risk necessary to get your mind in sync with mine. I was assuming the role of your personal trainer and I was committed to pushing you to the limits. Thanks for not getting frustrated or giving up.

Now the ball is in your court. If you've read this book and absorbed all of these thoughts, philosophies, and techniques, what's next? Nearly half the pages you've just finished reading were challenging you to make decisions and to take action. In my experience I have found the real losers in life were those people who died while they were still getting ready to get ready. Whether you already have an existing business you need to grow or whether you are thinking about starting a new business, procrastination and excuses are your worst enemies. Complacency is fatal.

Don't wait until everything is "perfect" either. It will never be precisely the right time if you are just sitting around waiting for the right time to magically appear. Just start doing it now and perfect it later. Fire before you aim and then adjust your sights. Make adjustments as you grow. You are going to make mistakes and you're going to correct them and survive through them. I view every mistake I have ever made in business as an investment. Knowing beyond a shadow of a doubt what doesn't work has helped to make me a wealthy man.

Stop asking everyone else what you should do with your life. You've already done that too much. This is your time, your life, your dreams. It's time to be true to your heart and to follow those dreams. I am not urging you to be irresponsible or to break commitments or to abandon those you love. I am saying you already know the right thing to do. If you are only in the idea stage, then you need to solidify your dream first. Work out the details in your mind and on paper. That process, in itself, is an action.

I want to hear from you. More than the money…more than any fame or success…I wrote this book to help others. Nothing on Earth would give me more satisfaction than knowing something you got here caused your life to be better for the experience.

It is my sincere hope that one day soon we'll be celebrating your success. Good luck!

Bibliography

Attard, Janet. *The Home Office and Small Business Answer Book: Solutions to the Most Frequently Asked Questions about Starting and Running Your Business.* New York: Owl Books, 2000.

Blanchard, Kenneth H. and Spencer Johnson. *The One Minute Manager.* New York: Berkley Publishing Group, 1983.

Carnegie, Dale. *How to Win Friends and Influence People.* New York: Pocket Books, 1998.

Covey, Stephen R. *The 7 Habits of Highly Effective People.* New York: Simon and Schuster, 1990.

Fridson, Martin S. *How to Be a Billionaire: Proven Strategies from the Titans of Wealth.* New York: John Wiley & Sons, 2000.

Hill, Napoleon. *Think and Grow Rich.* New York: Fawcett Book Group, 1996.

Johnson, Spencer, M.D. *Who Moved My Cheese? An Amazing Way to Deal with Change in Your Work and in Your Life.* New York: Putnam Publishing Group, 1998.

Kimbro, Dennis. *Think and Grow Rich: A Black Choice.* New York: Fawcett Book Group, 1992.

Kiyosaki, Robert T. *Rich Dad, Poor Dad: What the Rich Teach Their Kids About Money That the Poor and Middle Class Do Not.* New York: Warner Books, 2000.

Levinson, Jay Conrad. *The Guerilla Marketing Handbook.* Boston: Houghton Mifflin Co, 1995.

McCormack, Mark H. *What They Don't Teach You at Harvard Business School.* New York: Bantam Doubleday Dell Publishing, 1988.

———, *What They Still Don't Teach You at Harvard Business School.* New York: Bantam Doubleday, 1990.

Popeil, Ron, with Jefferson Graham. *The Salesman of the Century.*

Rudl, Corey. *The Insider Secrets to Marketing Your Business on the Internet.* Blaine, Washington: Internet Marketing Center, 2000.

Sewell, Carl, and Paul B. Brown. *Customers for Life: How to Turn That Onetime Buyer into a Lifetime Customer.* New York: Pocket Books, 1998.

Stanley, Thomas J. *The Millionaire Mind.* Kansas City, Missouri: Andrews McMeel Publishing, 2000.

Index

Give the Gift of

The Prosperity
EQUATION

The Entrepreneur's Road Map to Wealth

to Your Friends and Colleagues

CHECK YOUR LEADING BOOKSTORE OR ORDER HERE

❏ **YES**, I want _____ copies of ***The Prosperity Equation***: *The Entrepreneur's Road Map to Wealth* at $19.95 each, plus $4 shipping per book (Georgia residents please add $1.20 sales tax per book). Canadian orders must be accompanied by a postal money order in U.S. funds. Allow 15 days for delivery.

❏ **YES**, I am interested in having James A. Ziegler speak or give a seminar to my company, association, school, or organization. Please send information.

My check or money order for $_____ is enclosed.

Please charge my   ❏ Visa   ❏ MasterCard
                      ❏ Discover   ❏ American Express

Name _____

Organization _____

Address _____

City/State/Zip _____

Phone_____ E-mail _____

Card # _____

Exp. Date_____ Signature _____

Please make your check payable and return to:

Peach State Press

1244 Beaver Ruin Road, #300 • Norcross, GA 30093

Call your credit card order to: 800-726-0510

Fax: 770-921-6323